100 ESSENTIAL NEW ZEALAND Golf Holes

First published in 2008 by Awa Press,
16 Walter Street, Wellington, New Zealand

For photography credits, see pages 226–227

A CIP catalogue record for this book is available
from the National Library of New Zealand

ISBN 978-0-9582750-8-8

Book design by Fortyfive Design, Wellington
Typeset by Jenn Hadley, Wellington
Printed by Everbest Printing Company, China
This book is typeset in Minion

www.awapress.com

Tom Hyde

100 ESSENTIAL NEW ZEALAND

Golf Holes

AWA PRESS

Contents

Acknowledgements 8

Map of New Zealand 10

1 The 1st at Houhora 12

2 The 7th at Carrington 14

3 The 15th at Carrington 16

4 The 5th at Kauri Cliffs 18

5 The 7th at Kauri Cliffs 20

6 The 14th at Kauri Cliffs 22

7 The 6th at Kaitaia 24

8 The 13th at Kerikeri 26

9 The 11th at Waitangi 28

10 The 15th at Whangarei 30

11 The 14th at Sherwood Park 32

12 The 16th at Gulf Harbour 34

13 The 17th at South Head 38

14 The 10th at Helensville 40

15 The 3rd at Huapai 42

16 The 12th at Muriwai 44

17 The 1st at Redwood Park 47

18 The 13th at Titirangi 49

19 The 18th at Maungakiekie 52

20 The 8th at Akarana 54

21 The 3rd at Remuera 56

22 The 15th at Howick 58

23 The 11th at Formosa 61

24 The 16th at Formosa 63

25	The 7th at The Grange	*65*
26	The 4th at Manukau	*67*
27	The 12th at Clarks Beach	*69*
28	The 4th at Pukekohe	*70*
29	The 8th at Thames	*72*
30	The 17th at Lakes Resort	*74*
31	The 17th at Omokoroa	*76*
32	The 12th at Tauranga	*78*
33	The 18th at Mount Maunganui	*80*
34	The 6th at Te Puke	*82*
35	The 13th at Whakatane	*85*
36	The 14th at Ohope	*87*
37	The 16th at Springfield	*89*
38	The 14th at Arikikapakapa	*92*
39	The 1st at Horsham Downs	*94*
40	The 18th at St Andrews	*96*
41	The 18th at Narrows	*98*
42	The 4th at Cambridge	*101*
43	The 6th at Waitomo	*103*
44	The 14th at Poverty Bay	*105*
45	The 16th at Maraenui	*107*
46	The 16th at Waiohiki	*109*
47	The 6th at Cape Kidnappers	*111*
48	The 13th at Cape Kidnappers	*113*
49	The 14th at Cape Kidnappers	*115*
50	The 17th at Hastings	*117*

Contents

51	The 6th at Wairakei	119
52	The 14th at Wairakei	122
53	The 18th at Centennial	124
54	The 3rd at Kinloch	126
55	The 18th at Kinloch	128
56	The 4th at Tarrangower	130
57	The 17th at Ngamotu	132
58	The 15th at Westown	135
59	The 10th at Manaia	137
60	The 3rd at Belmont Links	139
61	The 18th at Rangatira	141
62	The 7th at Rangitikei	144
63	The 13th at Hokowhitu	147
64	The 15th at Levin	149
65	The 18th at Paraparaumu Beach	151
66	The 15th at Titahi	154
67	The 14th at Mahunga	157
68	The 11th at Lansdowne	159
69	The 3rd at Martinborough	161
70	The 1st at Te Marua	163
71	The 10th at Heretaunga	165
72	The 10th at Hutt	167
73	The 1st at Miramar	170
74	The 6th at Nelson	172
75	The 13th at Greenacres	174
76	The 11th at Clearwater	176

77	The 1st at Windsor	*179*
78	The 4th at Shirley	*181*
79	The 18th at Avondale	*183*
80	The 2nd at Russley	*184*
81	The 11th at Templeton	*186*
82	The 3rd at Akaroa	*188*
83	The 16th at Terrace Downs	*190*
84	The 8th at Greymouth	*192*
85	The 14th at Hokitika	*194*
86	The 10th at St Andrews	*196*
87	The 17th at North Otago	*198*
88	The 11th at Balmacewen	*200*
89	The 9th at Chisholm Park	*202*
90	The 15th at St Clair	*204*
91	The 11th at Cromwell	*206*
92	The 13th at Arrowtown	*208*
93	The 18th at Arrowtown	*210*
94	The 18th at Millbrook	*212*
95	The 5th at Kelvin Heights	*214*
96	The 10th at Kelvin Heights	*216*
97	The 8th at Jack's Point	*218*
98	The 10th at Te Anau	*220*
99	The 14th at Otatara	*222*
100	The 11th at Oreti Sands	*223*
Photography Credits		*226*

Acknowledgements

The golf holes featured in this book were selected sometimes for their natural features and design, sometimes for their stunning location, and sometimes because there was a good story associated with them. If you are looking for a different kind of guide to New Zealand golf, here are 100 holes that are worth talking about, and which I guarantee you will find interesting, challenging – and, I hope, enjoyable – to play.

There is a wealth of choice for golfers in New Zealand, with a well-kept golf course of some description in every town and off every country road. This ready accessibility to the game has led to New Zealand producing some exceptional golfers, with recent high-flyers including Michael Campbell, winner of the 2005 United States Open, and Danny Lee, winner of the 2008 US Amateur Championship, and the number one amateur player in the world as this book went to press.

In making these selections and researching each hole I have relied on a combination of sources, from my own experience playing the holes to information from other golfers, golf media and the internet. Most of all, though, I have relied on the recollections and insights of the following people, whom I wish to thank for their time and contributions:

Paul Barlow, Rodger Bartlett, Miles Bentley, Don Betts, Jeanette Boswell, Brian Boys, John Brooks, Sheryl Brownlee, Greg Bryan, Sandra Buchanan, Jan Canute, Jeremy Carlsen, Peter Cassidy, Derek Clarke, Nick Cooper, Winston Cooper, Anabel Darby, Nick Davey, Dawn Dowling, Kay Ebborn, Richard Ellis, David Faulls, Wayne Fowler, Robin Fulton, Dale Futcher, George Girling, Murray Glasgow, Neil Grant, Patricia Griffin, Matt Hamill, Glenda

Hardacre, Doug Harradine, Brian Hawker, Peter Hay, Bruce Hicks, Bob Hilt, Don Hope, Bob Howitt, Graham Hughes, Trevor Irving, Grant James, Stuart Jones, Brian Jopson, Pip King, Jill Kirby, Rhonda Kite, Bruce Klue, Lindsay Knight, Peter Lampp, Tom Long, Murray McAlley, Dave McCallum, Peter McGee, Murray MacGibbon, Allan McKay, Geoff McNally, Kevin May, Brian Moore, Bruce More, Craig Mowat, Dean Murphy, NZGA, Debbie Ogilvy, Paul Ogilvy, Jack Oliver, Brenda Ormsby, Tom Penrose, Betsy Pie, Keith Plowman, Noel Preston, Janet Rae, Scott Riordan, Evan Robb, Dennis Rollinson, Dr John Rouse, Bob Schumacher, Damon Selwyn, Barry Shannon, Allan Shaw, Graham Sherlock, Jerry Shih, Burton Shipley, Waihoroi Shortland, Rob Sinkinson, David Smith, Patrick Smith, Lorraine Stewart, Sonny Tekanawa, Brendan Telfer, Clive Thompson, Michael Thompson, Stuart Thompson, Bruce Tourell, Jamie Troughton, Neil Tuffery, Don Warner, Rhys Watkins, Andrew Whiley, Ross Willcocks, and Neil Woodbury.

Finally, I would like to thank Mary Varnham, Sarah Bennett, Hannah Bennett and the rest of the team at Awa Press for their sterling effort editing the manuscript and working overtime to make this book successful.

North Island

South Island

The 1st at Houhora

AGATHIS AUSTRALIS, the New Zealand kauri, is one of the world's most remarkable trees. For starters, the family it comes from is older than the cathedrals of Europe, older than the Roman Empire. It's even older than my next-door neighbour and he's still going on about 'the bloody Prussians'. According to *Te Ara – The Encyclopaedia of New Zealand*, the kauri first appeared in New Zealand about twenty million years ago, and is the most southern growing of a species that can be found across the belly of Melanesia and South-east Asia from New Guinea to Malaysia.

Before Europeans arrived, these monster trees of New Zealand's far north covered more than 10,000 square kilometres. However, it quickly turned out that, being very tall and very straight, they were excellent for ships' masts and other purposes, so acreage was quickly reduced.

Kauri are surprisingly vulnerable because they have a shallow root system. In fact, one theory as to why kauri logs still remain buried today is that at some stage, say 50,000 years ago, the water level rose high enough to weaken the root system, leaving the trees to topple over into swamps.

What has this to do with golf? Absolutely nothing – but travel to the far north and you'll find the legacy of this process at a number of tourist stops, including the Wagener Museum in Houhora, not far from the golf course.

Houhora Harbour

The Houhora Golf Club is not flash, in fact it can be swampy, but it has the distinction of being the northernmost course in the country. The par-4 first hole has an elevated tee, the highest on this idiosyncratic 18-tee, nine-hole course. In other words, the first and tenth greens are one and the same.

Maybe it's the harbour, or nearby Ninety Mile Beach, or a combination of both, but playing here is charming. On weekdays it is likely the modest clubhouse will be locked up and silent, and there'll be no one about. Leave the green fee in the honesty box.

info

The 1st
Par 4
345 metres

Houhora Golf Club
Far North Road
Houhora
Tel (09) 409 8266
houhoragolfclub@paradise.net.nz

The 7th at Carrington

TALK ABOUT CARRINGTON and you used to be talking about a psychiatric hospital in Auckland. Hospital records may even show a golfer or two signing into its acute admission ward: golf is a game that drives some people crazy.

Unwittingly, the American billionaire who built this resort gave it the same name, so at the beginning telling someone you were going to check into Carrington for the weekend raised more than a few eyebrows, until it was made clear you were talking about the lodge at the tip of the Karikari Peninsula in the far north: a rustic 3,000-acre Black Angus cattle farm with an award-winning winery and a scenic 18-hole golf course. For the record, the owner, Paul Kelly, named the place after his daughter.

Furthermore, the par-3 seventh hole here is truly one of the best short holes in the North Island, for it plays over picturesque wetlands to a large, severely sloping green that rises up beyond a row of mature, too-dense-to-find-your-ball flax.

This is also one of the most deceptive par-3 holes around. Time and time again, I've seen players think they have the measure of it. They read a scorecard that says it is 165 metres or so from the tips. They take an iron from their bag and give their new top-of-the-line ten-dollar ball a good whack, only to watch the white orb fall short and disappear into the flax.

Or the ball reaches the green, and the player watches helplessly as it rolls back down into water.

In 2003 American golf course designer Matt Dye reshaped this course somewhat from its original form, but most of that work happened on the back nine. The seventh remains in its original form. Call it mental if you wish, but I've seen players hit three straight shots into the water here because they just can't accept that the best way to play this par 3 is to leave their ego in the bag.

info

The 7th
Par 3
165 metres

Carrington Resort
Matai Bay Road
Karikari Peninsula
RD3, Kaitaia
Tel (09) 408 7222
www.heritagehotels.co.nz/Carrington-Resort

The 15th at Carrington

DESIGNER MATT DYE, in his first solo project, did a superb job shaping the back nine here into an open, scenic, seaside links, where the best sea view happens at the 15th tee.

The hole is a par 4 that plays over a ravine and down a hill. The bush-clad ravine makes this hole especially interesting without being threatening, even for the average player. It's not a long carry, and because it plays downhill any half decent tee shot will carry it, and wind up in a good position to score par.

Put another way, some golf holes are especially scenic but there's a price to pay for that if you screw up. Usually it's lost strokes and a lost ball. This hole affords a terrific coastal view without being vicious.

The view from the tee takes in Rangaunu Bay and Mount Camel, a distinctive, volcanic hill, and, on the clearest of days, North Cape. After losing your ball in the water at the 7th and then making the long, arduous climb up the testy par-5 14th, this hole should make you feel good about yourself again. Most of us who play this unpredictable game are hacks who never really know for certain where our tee shots will go when we hit them. But we do play downhill with more confidence than uphill, ravine or no ravine.

info

The 15th
Par 4
403 metres

Carrington Resort
Matai Bay Road
Karikari Peninsula
RD3, Kaitaia
Tel (09) 408 7222
www.heritagehotels.co.nz/Carrington-Resort

The 5th at Kauri Cliffs

WHEN AMERICAN DESIGNER DAVID HARMAN dreamed up what I see as one of the top five golf courses in New Zealand, he spared not a thought for those of us who fear sharp cliffs and steep drop-offs. Anyone who believes golf is not a mental game needs their head examined, for sooner or later The Fear beats you.

The Fear inhibits the golf swing more than anything I can think of. Feeling afraid of your ability, not trusting yourself, can turn the backswing to mush, the downswing into an exercise in uncertainty. The result is anything from a shank to a divot deep enough to dig bones.

Play the fifth hole at Kauri Cliffs and you'll get the idea. Or am I projecting? I've played the hole five times, and five times the first ball I hit fell short and was lost to that godforsaken ravine that stretches across the abyss between the tee and the green.

The last time I truly believed I could get it done with a 4-iron from the white tee, just 130 metres away. But my tee shot fell short *again*, and the only saving grace was that this time I was experienced enough to use an old ball not worth the risk I'd have to incur to get it back.

This is one of the best par 3s in the land, so I shall never wimp out and play it safe to the left, where there is a generous landing area, from whence one could get up-and-down for par. That would be a coward's way out. So no, I will always go straight for the pin here, wherever it may be placed on the slick two-tiered green.

In golf the best way of overcoming The Fear is to face up to it and know that, no matter how many lost balls it takes, it can be done. At least that's what I keep telling myself.

info

The 5th
Par 3
130 metres

Kauri Cliffs
Matauri Bay Road
Matauri Bay
Tel (09) 407 0060
www.kauricliffs.com

Golfing at Kauri Cliffs has an added frisson: the chance to catch up on a significant event in New Zealand history. On July 10, 1985, Greenpeace vessel *Rainbow Warrior*, on its way to protest against French nuclear tests at Mururoa Atoll, was blown up in Auckland Harbour by French agents. In 1987 the ship was laid to rest in the Cavalli Islands, the backdrop to this beautiful golf course, and it is now a divers' mecca.

The 7th at Kauri Cliffs

WHAT A SMALL REMOTE ISLAND COUNTRY can achieve when an American billionaire turns up. When this internationally acclaimed golf course and luxury lodge opened in 2000, it dramatically raised the standard of the golf holiday in New Zealand.

From the impeccable condition of the course eleven months of the year (it is often closed for a month in winter to recover) to its efficient support services, which include fine food and five-star cottages for overnight stays, Kauri Cliffs has inspired the opening of other luxury golf resorts elsewhere in the country, and forced existing ones to pick up their game.

Kauri Cliffs is a course every passionate golfer must try to play before they die. Since it opened a decade ago it's seen the likes of Michael Campbell and Fred Couples playing a match for the long-running show *Shell's Wonderful World of Golf*, not to mention American pop star Justin Timberlake.

Once the green fee here required the average golfer to take out a second mortgage, but in recent years a rise in fees at other resorts has made Kauri Cliffs appear less expensive. Even some New Zealanders can now afford to play here, and it's worth the time and expense, trust me, because this course is situated above one of the most spectacular coastlines in the country. It remains exclusive, however, so if they don't want you, the private gate, rustic and charming as it is, will not open.

The 7th is a par 3 that, at 201 metres long, is in every way as scary as the 5th hole – only here The Fear comes with an extraordinary view down to the Cavalli Islands and back to Takau Bay. This makes it among the best par-3 holes in the land. To say this hole is challenging is like saying Mount Everest is challenging. The distance, and the extreme drop-off between the tee and the green, leave most players feeling a little weak in the knees.

info

The 7th
Par 3
201 metres
Kauri Cliffs
Matauri Bay Road
Matauri Bay
Tel (09) 407 0060
www.kauricliffs.com

The 14th at Kauri Cliffs

THE STATE OF FLORIDA may have more golf courses per square mile than any other state or country in the world. It is even shaped like a golf club. Orange groves, alligators, mega beaches and hotels, Disney World, hurricanes, political corruption and a zillion golf courses – that's Florida.

And why not a zillion golf courses? In spite of the occasional big blow, the skies are clear and the temperature hovers around 25°C, making the climate perfect for golf. They have also made Florida a showpiece of golf-course architecture. How many ways are there to build a golf course? Zillions of course. And among the best designers was the late David Harman.

Harman worked out of Orlando. He was one of the best because he learned from the best, including Jack Nicklaus, Arnold Palmer and Tom Fazio. And, like them, he built courses that are popular because they challenge the hotshot and the hack equally.

Harman designed Shingle Creek, a flash Orlando course attached to a luxury hotel, and while the hotel is fine, the course is regarded as one of the most difficult in Florida – and given the number of courses there are in Florida, that's meaningful.

Harman also designed Kauri Cliffs. My guess is that the owner, Julian Robertson, who knows a thing or two about golf courses himself, gave him a free hand, because Kauri Cliffs is at once the most spectacular

golf course in the country and one of the most difficult.

Kauri Cliffs is seductive, a siren that lulls you into a free-spirited state of mind, to the point where it doesn't matter that you just lost your fifth ball of the day over the edge at the 14th. All that matters is this: You are here.

info

The 14th
Par 3
116 metres

Kauri Cliffs
Matauri Bay Road
Matauri Bay
Tel (09) 407 0060
www.kauricliffs.com

The 14th is a 116-metre par 3, played directly toward the shimmering sea. On a kauri stump behind the tee Julian Robertson has placed a plaque in memory of David Harman, who passed away before his time.

The 6th at Kaitaia

AHIPARA, FIFTEEN KILOMETRES WEST OF KAITAIA, describes itself as the adventure capital of the north. And for all that goes on here – from horse-trekking to quad-biking to surfcasting to making oneself nauseous rolling down dunes off Ninety Mile Beach – why not?

For those who play golf, though, the best adventure is not bungy-jumping from a helicopter or kayaking over a waterfall, but playing 'The Drop', the par-3 sixth hole at the Kaitaia Golf Club – which is actually at Ahipara, right next to the beach.

'The Drop' is only 114 metres long, and on the calmest of days my

grandmother could have made par. All you have to do is coax an easy wedge on to the green, two-putt for par, and move on. On days like that it is truly what the scorecard says it is, the No. 15 stroke hole, if you accept that stroke ratings accurately indicate degree of difficulty.

info

The 6th
Par 3
114 metres

Kaitaia Golf Club
Takahe Street
Ahipara
Tel (09) 409 4833
kaitaia@golf.co.nz

On days when there's no wind they probably do. But this course sits in a stunning location at the southern end of Ninety Mile Beach, with a wind-provoking mountain tossed into the mix for good measure. So while Ahipara may be fantastic if your game is windsurfing, if your game is golf playing 'The Drop' from the highest tee in the far north, face on to gale-force winds, with a fine sea view, can be just as much fun: your ball sails off faster than anyone on a board sail.

The 13th at Kerikeri

FREE-ASSOCIATE WITH 'KERIKERI' and the first images that come to mind will probably be citrus fruit and the Stone Store, one of New Zealand's oldest buildings, although some may think of the even older Kemp House, built in 1822, and others (with an sense of impending doom) will recall the flood of 1981. But I doubt that anyone but the guy who scored a 10 on the short, dead-easy par-3 thirteenth hole at the Kerikeri Golf Club will think, 'That wretched golf course.' His name shall remain anonymous.

The Stone Store

So how does someone score a 10 on the 13th at Kerikeri? It is hard to fathom when you consider that it is the No. 18 stroke hole – in other words, the easiest hole on the course. It's also one of the prettiest, which is saying something because this course is blessed with a number of bucolic fairways and greens. But at the 13th there is that damnable water hazard and those three sand traps, and it doesn't seem to matter that they are clearly visible from the tee high

above the green, or that the hole is only 100 metres long: you score a 10 by knocking your first tee shot into one of the two small ponds.

You whack the next shot into the other pond and then, with your fifth shot from the tee, the ball trickles into the sand trap. It takes you two swings to get it out of the bunker before you three-putt … for a 10. That's when you remind yourself that there are only five holes to play and many bars and cafés waiting out on Kerikeri Road.

info

The 13th
Par 3
100 metres

Kerikeri Golf Club
Golf View Road
Kerikeri
Tel (09) 407 8837
www.kerikerigolf.co.nz

The 11th at Waitangi

THE WAITANGI PENINSULA may have been lost to Maori after the signing of the Treaty in 1840 but, luckily for those of us who like to hang out there, in 1932 a large chunk of it fell into the hands of Charles Bathurst, also known as Lord Bledisloe, the governor-general of New Zealand from 1930 to 1935.

After Bledisloe purchased the thousand acres, he donated it to the 'inhabitants of New Zealand', under the supervision of the Waitangi National Trust. The trust's board, which includes descendants and representatives of Treaty signatories, has done a splendid job looking after it all these years, and is still today responsible for looking after the grounds, the gardens – and the golf course.

There's nothing to suggest that Lord Bledisloe played golf. He may have played a round or two somewhere, perhaps in the Old Country, but when it came to sport his true passion was rugby. The feverish Bledisloe Cup rivalry between the All Blacks and the Wallabies is just one of his legacies. So his generous gift of such a precious piece of land – at a time when colonials still celebrated Empire Day – is remarkable.

The golf course opened in 1944 and it reflects a more modest time in the Bay of Islands, before the region became swept up by tourism. The course designer's name is surely buried in records somewhere. Perhaps he was a Ministry of Works engineer who played golf.

He did a splendid job.

Some who have played here will tell you about the 10th hole, a par 3 with a panoramic view: on a bright day in summer Onewhero Bay and the islands are transformed into a glistening jewel of emerald and blue. That's nice, but the truth is that no matter what the weather, the par-4 eleventh, sweeping down and around toward the bay, is a better golf hole. Indeed, it is one of the best par-4s in Northland.

info

The 11th
Par 4
366 metres

Waitangi Golf Club
Tau Henare Drive
Paihia
Tel (09) 402 7713
www.waitangigolf.co.nz

The 15th at Whangarei

IF ARBOREAL ODDITIES INTEREST YOU, go to the Whangarei Golf Club, where you'll find the club's signature tree: a split pine. This tree was barely older than a sapling when it was struck by lightning, and today its two trunks resemble giant parentheses. There's a photo of it on the club scorecard.

Unfortunately the tree does not come into play unless you happen to be a truly terrible player, so I'm left to write about the par-3 fifteenth, one of the most pleasant-looking but devil-to-play golf holes in Northland. This hole is picturesque to say the least, with its raised tee, cabbage trees, nikau palms, duck pond, and three nicely placed pot bunkers. Even if you avoid all of that you must still contend with a three-tiered green.

It is only 112 metres across the pond to the green from the white tee, and just 92 metres across from the yellow tee, but, like a stereotypical female movie star, this golf hole is lovely to look at but sometimes hell to live with.

Just ask the woman whose name was strangely hard to track down after she scored a 14 here. How many balls did she lose to the pond? Your guess is as good as mine. It wasn't the first 14 scored at that hole, and others have scored more, but for this particular golfer that score, totally off the charts for any one hole, compounded her frustration: at this same hole a few years before she had scored a hole-in-one.

The 15th has multiple personalities, and on any given day, even if it happens to be perfect weather for golf – calm, not too hot – there is no telling what can happen. On one day a year the club members entirely give up trying to reach the green in one, and for charity everyone aims for a row boat anchored in the middle of the pond.

info

The 15th
Par 3
112 metres

Whangarei Golf Club
Denby Crescent
Tikipunga
Whangarei
Tel (09) 437 0775
www.whangareigolfclub.co.nz

The 14th at Sherwood Park

I RISK CONTROVERSY, but what would life be without it? I nominate the Sherwood Park Golf Club as the best golf course in Whangarei, a notch above both Northland Golf Club and Whangarei Golf Club at Mount Denby.

Sherwood Park is classic countryside, in a way the other two are not. With its stone walls, it resembles an English country scene. Equestrian paddocks nearby are a perfect fit. They could change the name of this golf club to John Constable Park and get away with it.

This club had humble beginnings, as they say. It started around 1950 as a nine-holer, but by 1967 it had became so popular that a big new chunk of farm land was acquired. The course lies below the Maunu volcanic cone, and its lush greenery is helped along by the rich soils and subtropical climate.

The 14th hole here is a par 3 across two small ponds to a green encircled by a fine grove of native trees – kauri, puriri and karaka among them.

For one of the club's annual tournaments a few years ago, on a fine October day, a Whangarei insurance company offered a $500 voucher to the first player who scored a hole-in-one at this hole. Cameron Barbour from Wellsford won, but there was controversy: was $500 worth of insurance enough for his feat? The 14th is 154 metres long, so simply reaching the green in one is a good shot for most of us. You may think

Barbour should have won full coverage on home and car for a year at least.

Whatever, the two ponds catch more balls being played down the 13th fairway than from tee-offs at the 14th, which may be why the club's members refer to these two holes as 'Amen Corner'. Okay, fine, this may be God's own country, but really at the 14th at Sherwood Park a good golf swing is more useful than prayer.

info

The 14th
Par 3
154 metres

Sherwood Park Golf Club
Millington Road
Maunu
Whangarei
Tel (09) 434 6900
www.sherwoodpark.nzgolf.net

The 16th at Gulf Harbour

THE WORLD CUP OF GOLF began in 1953 as the Canada Cup, for the simple reason that it was founded by a Canadian. John Jay Hopkins saw golf as a game that might improve relations among countries, but as the cup was first played during the Cold War it had little impact. Russians, after all, didn't play golf. Golf was bourgeois.

Golf is still bourgeois but that's beside the point. In the 1960s the Canada Cup became the World Cup, and in the early '90s the name was changed again, presumably for clarity – and so the organisers wouldn't be sued by FIFA, the football impresarios – to the World Cup of Golf.

International relations aside, the tournament has continued to be played in one location or another around the globe, depending on which private benefactor or sports marketing company can come up with the millions of dollars it takes to stage it. From 2007 to 2018 the venue will be the 216-hole Mission Hills Golf Club in Shenzhen, China.

In 1998 it was held at the Gulf Harbour Country Club, a development with a golf course, houses and a marina, at the tip of the Whangaparaoa Peninsula, thirty minutes drive north of Auckland.

While the tournament has often attracted more second-tier professionals than stars, in 1998 a handful of international golf stars did turn up – perhaps lured, as many people around the world are, by all the talk about the beauty of the country. And among the sightseeing pros was John Daly.

Daly had burst on to the international scene in 1991 when he won golf's fourth Major, the PGA Championship. He had not even been expected to play in the tournament. He was ninth on the list of alternates, which meant eight other players had to become ill or lose a family member or stub their big toe for Daly to get a tee time. But incredibly it happened. Nick Price withdrew at the very last minute, so late that none of the first eight alternates could make it.

Daly, a hard drinker at the time, drove through the night to make his tee time, then went on to win the championship by three shots. He instantly became one of the most popular sports personalities in the United States.

Daly wasn't at all like the privileged, private country club types who tended to dominate American golf. Nicknamed The Lion, not only was he a drinker, he was also overweight and a gambler, so regular people related to him.

And more than anyone who had ever played the game, Daly, with his enormous backswing, drove the ball longer than any other touring pro.

At the 1998 World Cup at Gulf Harbour, the question each day at the 16th tee was, 'Will JD go for it?' The 16th is a dramatic dog-leg right along a cliff top. Cut the corner and most players will lose their

ball to the sea. But not Daly. Each day he put on a show. One day he drove his tee shot out over the water and hooked it back on to the fairway. It was a drive of more than 250 metres across the abyss. The ball wound up just shy of the green in light rough, leaving many in the gallery stone silent, mouths hanging open.

info

The 16th
Par 4
405 metres

Gulf Harbour Country Club
Gulf Harbour Drive
Whangaparaoa Peninsula
Tel (09) 428 1380
www.ghcc.co.nz

The 17th at South Head

THERE'S A PRECIOUS PHOTO on the website of the South Head Golf Club showing Tiger Woods and Steve Williams sitting around with some of the members after a round of golf. This round, in April 2006, may be the only one Tiger has ever played where he was the caddy, not the player. He caddied for Williams, who makes his New Zealand home not far from here, and who is the club's official patron.

Steve Williams began caddying at the ripe old age of ten at the Paraparaumu Beach Golf Club, where his father was a member. By his own account, he was a 2 handicap by the age of thirteen, but he enjoyed caddying more. Before he knew it, his father had arranged for him to caddy for Peter Thomson, the winner of five British Opens and arguably Australia's greatest player, at the New Zealand Open at Heretaunga.

Williams pursued caddying like no New Zealander had ever done. He went to Europe, where he worked for ten years – six for Greg Norman – before working for Ray Floyd on the US PGA Tour.

In 1999 Tiger Woods called, and Williams' life, and the lives of all proud Kiwi golfers, has not been the same since. When you live so geographically removed from the United States, Europe and the heartbeat of golf, having a local boy make good is something to toast. Today, when he's not on tour, Williams is more likely to be driving a stock car than handling a golf club. Still, he managed to get in a round at South Head that day, with the greatest player in the world carrying his bag.

> **info**
>
> **The 17th**
> **Par 5**
> **382 metres**
>
> **South Head Golf Club**
> **1640 South Head Road**
> **Helensville**
> **Tel (09) 420 2838**
> **www.shgc.info**

'Eccles Highway', the name of the 17th hole here, is a tribute to Jack Eccles, the man who designed the course. Club legend has it that he took only two weeks and a few whiskies to get the job done.

To what extent you can see the influence of whisky on the layout of South Head remains a talking point, but whatever it was that inspired Eccles, at the 17th he got it right. At 382 metres, it is one of the shortest par-5 holes in the country, but it's also one of the prettiest, with a bank of trees and stone, and a series of bunkers down the right side of a fairway that slopes right to left into a grove of trees – trees that in autumn erupt in colour. Before teeing off, pause a moment to take in the sweeping view of Kaipara Harbour.

The 10th at Helensville

THE OLD BOYS, still crazy after all these years, had just completed a game of basketball in the weekly Wednesday night competition at the North Shore Events Centre when Mark Arblaster collapsed. Even Bruce Twaddle, a brilliant doctor and veteran player – the one man on the scene with the knowledge and experience to revive him – was unable to do so. Mark, just forty-nine, had died, leaving family and friends, and many other people who knew of him, stunned.

Arblaster had represented the North Shore, and more lately North Harbour, in basketball and cricket. He was still active in both as a player, coach and volunteer organiser at the time of his death. Married with two children, he had never rowed competitively, but when his son Simon took up the sport at Westlake Boys High School and it was discovered the school had no coach, he volunteered to do that too.

Mark Arblaster lived on a block of land at Dairy Flat. Each year he hosted an annual 'golf tournament'. He mowed nine so-called 'greens', and created 'holes' where to score par commonly meant playing a shot off the barn, or through it, or over it. Ball and club selection was limited and beer-in-hand was a rule strictly enforced. No beer, no golf.

info

The 10th
Par 3
138 metres

Helensville Golf Club
197 Peak Road, RD 2
Helensville
Tel (09) 420 5454
www.helensville.nzgolf.net

Now he was gone.

The Old Boys rallied, organising a Mark Arblaster Memorial Trust golf tournament, which takes place annually at Helensville. Memorial golf tournaments, usually raising money for a good cause, are not uncommon. Another well-known name in New Zealand basketball, Alan Bland, is remembered in a similar way by his former teammates and friends in Wellington. There is a golf tournament in memory of the late All Black Lin Colling, and another, at Waimarama each January, for actor Bruno Lawrence.

On the day, it's not who wins and who loses that matters. In the Arblaster tournament, the format is 'Ambrose' – a team of four playing alternate shots. Afterwards, a raffle is held and prizes handed out for Longest Drive and Closest to the Pin.

The 10th hole at Helensville is a medium length par 3 that creates more havoc than it should. Hacks like me commonly pull the ball left into a grove of trees, or slice it right down a steep slope.

However, someone always gets it right, and with that goal in mind everyone puts five bucks into a can to enter Closest to the Pin. The best shot wins a prize, and money raised for the trust supports junior sport on the North Shore.

The 3rd at Huapai

AT AROUND THREE O'CLOCK on the afternoon of December 23, 1991, as the rest of the world was spinning out of control in a mad pre-Christmas dash, I was standing, calmly detached from it all, on the tee at the 18th hole at the Huapai Golf Club.

Before taking our final tee shots of the day, Mark Leishman and I were talking about dogs. Mark, an independent television producer, was planning a dog show, and so our conversation that day ranged from media gossip (who was having sex with whom) to border collies.

The 18th hole at Huapai in 1991 is today the third, but the change was more in number than design: it remains a 120-metre par 3 to a flat green sitting up slightly higher than the tee. It is a short hole, but it has a sand trap directly in front.

Mark said he had a sponsor lined up for the show, and as I pulled an 8-iron from my bag I thought: A dog show, great idea! Everyone loves dogs. As I bent down to stick a tee in the ground I thought of Brownie, our family beagle when I was growing up.

With the iron in my grip I set up over the ball in my usual inconsistent stance – like most hacks, my 'set-up' is never the same from one tee to the next. But this time I made good contact with the ball. It felt right. It sounded right. And most of all it flew incredibly straight.

When I was a child, my brother and I shared a room. One dark summer's night I woke to a strange sound. Something was in the room:

I could hear it growling. I was seven and I knew what it was – a Martian! I had seen the headline in a tabloid newspaper: 'Martians have invaded Earth'. Now they were here, in Celoron, New York.

I jumped out of bed and ran screaming down the hall, waking my parents and sister, and causing my older brother to shake his fist at me. My sister, the smartest of us all, rapidly figured out that the growling I had heard was Brownie snoring at the foot of my brother's bed.

All of that came rushing back to me as my ball plopped on to the green directly in line with the pin and took a few small hops before it disappeared into the hole.

info

The 3rd
Par 3
120 metres

Huapai Golf Club
1261 Coatesville-Riverhead Highway
Kumeu
Tel (09) 412 8809
www.huapaigolf.co.nz

The 12th at Muriwai

HARVEY PENICK WAS A GREAT TEACHER, not just of golf but of life: his approach to the game was built on a philosophy of living. Penick coached the University of Texas golf team for years. He was also the pro at Austin Country Club.

Penick's coaching and noble patience produced some of the best players in American golf, among them United States Open winner Tom

Kite and Masters champion Ben Crenshaw. One of the most heartfelt moments in golf happened on the 18th green at Augusta National in 1995, when Crenshaw broke down after putting out to win the Masters the day after serving as a pall-bearer at Penick's funeral.

Penick compiled his instructional notes into a book called *Harvey Penick's Little Red Book*, which has become a staple on every dedicated golfer's bookshelf – for, like any book on life's lessons, it is best read more than once. In it Penick addresses each of the main technical issues, from how to grip a club to how to chip and putt, in his own soft and gentlemanly way.

Harvey Penick's advice about how to play on, and out of, sand is especially useful when playing the Muriwai Golf Club. The course here, being next to the beach, is built on sand. There's no way to avoid the

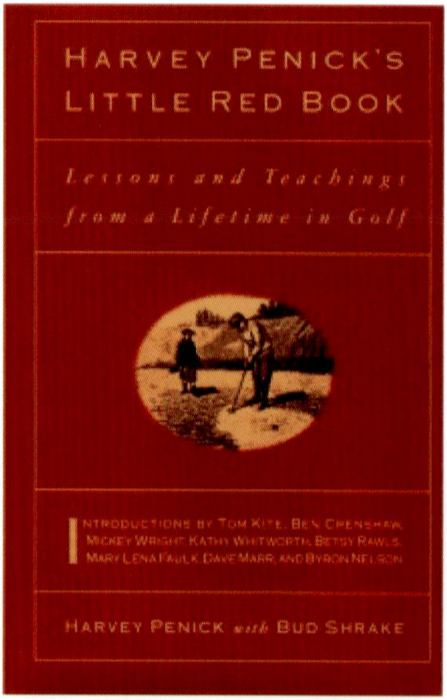

stuff, even on fairways. The sand traps are that heavy black west coast sand, so dense it should be mined (just kidding). The sand is the product of aeons of volcanic activity and is rich in iron and other minerals, hence its hue – and its appeal to mining companies, who have to be periodically repelled by the locals.

Two Penick tips come to mind on this course. One: Don't scoop the ball off a sandy fairway; try to pick it up clean. Two: Strike the sand close to the ball for longer shots, and further back from the ball for shorter ones.

info

The 12th
Par 5
452 metres

Muriwai Beach Golf Club
Coast Road
Muriwai
Tel (09) 411 8454
www.muriwaigolfclub.co.nz

With those simple thoughts in mind you may be ready for the par-5 twelfth at Muriwai – a hole that bends around right to left like a green banana. It's a golf hole that would be altogether easy to play were it not for the soft sand beneath a thin veil of grass and seven perfectly placed traps. Muriwai may be a seaside links but on the 12th hole, sheltered as it is by a grove of dense pine, it is not the wind but the sand that can drive a sane person crazy.

The 1st at Redwood Park

IT WAS WILLIAM J. LIBBY, professor of forests and genetics at the University of California at Berkeley, who told *The New York Times*: 'Redwood forests are particularly impressive in New Zealand.'

Libby would know. Apart from being a forest scientist and a board member of the Save-the-Redwoods League, he has been to Whakarewarewa Forest, also known as The Redwoods, near Rotorua and seen them for himself.

Redwoods are, in my view, the most impressive exotic New Zealand tree. They grow to more than a hundred metres tall with as much as a five-metre girth, and while any single tree can live as long as two thousand years, redwood ancestry goes back millions of years.

Redwoods were first planted in New Zealand in the early 1900s, although most of the ones that golfers (and non-golfers) enjoy at the Redwood Park Golf Course in Swanson appear to be younger.

The first hole here is one of the strangest opening holes in New Zealand golf. I mean, usually you expect the first to be reasonably short and straight, the fairway reasonably wide and flat, and the green with no more than one innocuous bunker. People are still waking up when they play the first hole.

But at Redwood Park the first, only 312 metres long, plays uphill, then breaks left at a ninety-degree angle. The elbow is about 200 metres out, which means that for many players only a good roll will

clear the corner, setting up a good look at the green – one that cannot be reached across the corner because of tall, impenetrable eucalyptus trees.

Still, this is one opening hole worth playing because it is the only first in New Zealand where you will tee off between two giant redwoods.

info

The 1st
Par 4
312 metres

Redwood Park Golf Club
13 Knox Road, Swanson
Auckland
Tel (09) 833 8253
www.nzgolfcourses.co.nz/redwoodpark

The 13th at Titirangi

AFTER COMPLETING HIS MEDICAL DEGREE and serving in the Boer War, Alister MacKenzie, born in Yorkshire in 1870, turned to designing golf courses. MacKenzie was influenced by his fellow designer and friend Harry Colt, but while Colt played golf, and played well, MacKenzie did not play at all. This was the central irony in the life of a man who became one of the greatest course designers of all time – one who is appreciated even more now that most golf courses built since the 1950s are more shaped than designed.

Monstrous earth-moving machines able to shift half of Scotland in a single day didn't exist in MacKenzie's time, so designers had to go with the flow, or rather the lay of the land. MacKenzie's 'naturalism', as it is sometimes called, is today viewed as an art form. Just ask any of the loyal members of the Alister MacKenzie Society of Great Britain and Ireland, a worldwide collection of disciples who study MacKenzie the way some people study the bible. In fact, they will tell you that when it comes to building golf courses Dr Alister MacKenzie *is* the bible.

In 1920 MacKenzie wrote *Golf Architecture*, one of the first books on golf course design. In it he described his approach this way:

'In discussing the need for simplicity of design, the chief object of every golf course architect worth his salt is to imitate the beauties of nature so closely as to make his work indistinguishable from nature itself.'

Titirangi is the only MacKenzie course in New Zealand and, despite the many modifications that have been made since the designer was here in 1926, it retains the simplicity and naturalism he originally created. Many MacKenzie disciples point to the four par-3 holes at Titirangi as classic MacKenzie, and that may be true, but my personal favourite is the par-5 thirteenth, known famously as 'Wrecker'. It ranks among the best par-5 holes in the land.

My guess is that at the 12th green the good doctor worked himself into a corner where he had little choice but to make the turn, back toward the clubhouse. The only option he had for the 13th hole, given the shape of the land, was to tee off to an elevated, hidden fairway running right to left, and over a gully with a pine tree rising up in the middle.

At least that's how it plays today. A series of sand traps lies front right of the green.

Five years after MacKenzie worked over Titirangi, he created Royal Melbourne, and two years later he completed Augusta National. Is it overstating the case to suggest that his success with those two world-famous courses was a product of the work he did here?

info

The 13th
Par 5
467 metres

Titirangi Golf Club
Links Road, New Lynn
Waitakere
Tel (09) 827 5749
www.titirangigolf.co.nz

The 18th at Maungakiekie

THE *GUINNESS BOOK OF WORLD RECORDS* has a long-winded category: 'The Most Times for a Golfer to Score Their Age and Below'.

Think about it. The idea of someone 'shooting their age' is not even imaginable until the age of sixty-five to seventy, and by then you have to count yourself lucky if you're playing golf at all.

No matter how you look at it, shooting your age is an exceptional feat. As of September 2008, the world record was allegedly held by Kermit Dannehl of the Ahwatukee Country Club in Phoenix, Arizona. From 1992 to 2007 Dannehl shot his age a remarkable 1,138 times.

However, the *Guinness Book of World Records* may have it wrong. At the time this book went to print, Keith Plowman, a member of the Maungakiekie Golf Club, had shot his age more times than this.

Given this hot tip, I called Plowman to find out if it were true. 'About how many times have you shot your age?' I asked.

My choice of 'about' upset him. He was, after all, eighty-nine years old and had been a member of the club for fifty-one years. 'I know *exactly* how many times,' he replied. '1,179!'

'That must surely be a New Zealand record,' I said, unaware how naïve I was.

'I would hope it's a world record,' he shot back.

I asked him for his favourite hole at Maungakiekie, but again I was being an idiot.

'The one I score best on!' he said.

Maungakiekie is the hilliest golf course in Auckland. It plays up-and-down like no other in the city. The 18th hole is a par 5 only 405 metres long from the white tee, but it plays straight up the hill. I'm sure the sight of the clubhouse at the top is what keeps some hacks tramping to the final putt.

The clubhouse is also where members have gathered many times to watch Keith Plowman make his way up (he said he uses a cart now) to see if, once again, he has extended his world record, whether the world knows it or not.

info

The 18th
Par 5
405 metres

Maungakiekie Golf Club
5 Anita Avenue
Mount Roskill
Auckland
Tel (09) 621 0090
www.maungakiekiegolf.co.nz

The 8th at Akarana

AUCKLAND'S NOTORIOUS TRAFFIC JAMS, which can occur even outside the usual rush hour, have forced the city to extend its motorways. To do that, some people and places have had to move, among them the Akarana Golf Club.

A new link to the motorway forced the club to redesign its golf course. The original first hole, a nasty little par 3 with a tall tree right in the line of fire, and bunkers on both sides of the green, had to be taken out – much to the delight, I would guess, of members who did not like starting their round with a bogey or worse.

To reshape the course, the club hired Chris Pitman, an accomplished English-born golf course architect who has been involved in the design and construction of golf courses in many different parts of the world. His work can be found in Portugal, France, Tunisia, Singapore and California, and now much of it can be seen in New Zealand, where he has worked on more than a half dozen courses in the greater Auckland region, including Akarana.

Founded in 1927, Akarana is one of Auckland's most established golf clubs. It was the home club of Jim Bissett, for whom the Bissett Shield, presented to the winner of the Auckland inter-club championship, is named. It's also the home of Vic Pirihi, who, before the coming of young guns such as Michael Campbell and Phil Tataurangi, was arguably the most accomplished Maori player, having won, among

other titles, the club championship twelve times. Pirihi is today a life member of the New Zealand Maori Golf Association, and an inspiration to Campbell, who began training under him in the Maori Junior Development Program in 1988, and three years later, as a 21-year-old, narrowly defeated him in the Maori Championship in Taupo.

info

The 8th
Par 3
175 metres

Akarana Golf Club
1388 Dominion Road
Mount Roskill
Auckland
Tel (09) 620 5461
www.akaranagolf.co.nz

Akarana was so well-established that change might never have happened had it not been for Auckland's traffic congestion. But like someone who discovers that life has got better since their divorce, the course now has a much better par-3 hole than the original, and now it's not the first but the 8th.

The hole is 175 metres long from the back tees, which for most hacks means a fairway wood, if not a driver. But then hacks would be silly to play this hole from the back tees. Still, what makes the eighth successful is the new water hazard, the new bunker, and a green noteworthy for being shaped like the head in Edvard Munch's famous painting 'The Scream', which is exactly what I've felt like doing here at times.

The 3rd at Remuera

ONE OF THE GREAT LEAPS FORWARD for New Zealand golf happened in the 1930s, when a number of new clubs opened. Why golf, famous for being a rich man's sport, became more popular during the Depression is a question for sociologists to sort out. Suffice to say that at a time when a lot of people were out of work, Remuera was one of a handful of newly formed clubs. A group of keen golfers leased 280 acres of scrubby land and set to work designing the course. Much of the hard yards were done by men on work relief schemes, and two courses evolved – one public and one private. From the mid '60s the current course began to emerge.

The myth surrounding the Remuera Golf Club has been that because it is located in Remuera, Auckland's famously expensive suburb, the club must be élitist. I haven't met all the members, so if someone told me there was a right old toff puffed up with his own importance I could believe it, but every time I've turned up here to play, people have been friendly and inviting and proud of the course, as they should be.

Remuera is as accessible as any club, providing you book a tee time in advance. And it has had a major facelift in recent years. A number of holes have been reworked, new bunkers have been installed and altogether the course is playing better than ever. The work has been done by the Canadian design firm Puddicombe Golf, which has a special talent for rebuilding holes in a way that can turn pumpkins

into gilded carriages.

Take the third hole for example. Once a medium length par 3 that played from an elevated tee to a plateau green, it had few redeeming features. Today it is one of the most scenic, and nerve-wracking, short holes in Auckland. Puddicombe made it look better and play more interestingly, starting with a water hazard framed by a stone retainer wall and new white-sand bunkers. It is simply a terrific golf hole.

info

The 3rd
Par 3
164 metres

Remuera Golf Club
120 Abbotts Way
Remuera
Auckland
Tel (09) 524 5147
www.remueragolfclub.com

The 15th at Howick

ON JANUARY 12, 1942 the New Zealand prime minister, Peter Fraser, cut the ribbon at the new Musick Point Air Radio Station, and with that launched a new phase in ship and air communications. Heaven only knows how anyone found the country before then.

The station was housed in an art deco building that remains today one of Auckland's little architectural gems. The service was managed by the Post Office and Civil Aviation before the government sold it to Telecom in the 1980s – by which time, as you might guess, it was no longer operating from the original building.

The site, however, continues to be known as Musick Point, after Captain Edwin Musick, the pilot of the Sikorsky S42B flying boat that made the first survey flight from the United States to New Zealand, touching down in Waitemata Harbour in March 1937.

The site was also a Maori pa until 1821, and the indentations of food pits can still be seen today. But any further archaeology of the site is not possible, because in 1934 the land – originally purchased from Maori by a missionary named William Fairburn for a price that included ninety blankets, twenty-four adzes and 900 pounds of tobacco – was bulldozed to make way for a nine-hole golf course.

The Howick Golf Club was open for play three years before Captain Musick landed in the harbour, so it's possible he saw the course from the air. If so, he would have observed a scratchy little nine-hole links.

info

The 15th
Par 4
388 metres

Howick Golf Club
Musick Point Road
Bucklands Beach
Manukau
Tel (09) 535 1001
www.howickgolf.co.nz

Over time this has become an 18-hole course with a terrific harbour vista.

The 15th tee shares that vista with two other tees (the 12th and 17th) and three greens (the 11th, 14th, and 16th), but the 15th hole has the most character. This is not because it's a whopping 388 metres from the white tee, making it the longest par 4 on the course, or because it is the No. 1 stroke hole. It's because of its fairway, which is shaped in a way that suggests someone was looking for a way to drain it naturally: it slopes away from a central ridge into rough on both sides.

Ten months after his historic flight, Captain Edwin Musick died, with his crew, when his flying boat crashed after taking off from Pago Pago in Samoa, bound for New Zealand. Peter Fraser, New Zealand's longest serving Labour prime minister until Helen Clark came along, died in 1950.

The 11th at Formosa

FORMOSA AUCKLAND, as distinct from its sister Formosa Taipei, opened in the late 1990s to great fanfare. Built by a tycoon from Taiwan, it instantly became one of the country's finest golf courses, located on one of Auckland's most scenic coastlines. From the patio of any of the fifty villas the view over the 11th fairway and out to Waitemata Harbour, with Rangitoto Island as a centrepiece, is very nice. And at over 6,600 metres the course is one of New Zealand's longest.

Soon after Formosa opened it hosted a New Zealand Open, but while the resort's wedding and conference business has continued to thrive, the golf course and recreation centre (squash, tennis, swimming pool and gym) have had their ups and downs. The New Zealand Open hasn't been back, and because of lack of adequate drainage, playing the course in winter can be like auditioning for a role in a remake of *All Quiet On The Western Front.*

Still, the course was designed by Bob Charles, and while what constitutes a great golf hole will always be a matter for debate, Formosa has at least two worth talking about. Sir Bob did not turn up at the grand opening, and to the best of my knowledge he's not been back at all, which may mean he's forgotten what a fine job he did with the back nine, starting with the par-3 eleventh.

The 11th at Formosa is a hole best played in the morning when the tide is full and sea is calm. Because the harbour forms the backdrop,

the hole is less attractive when the tide is out, to say nothing of when you find yourself playing into a headwind.

The hole is 207 metres long from the back tees. The green lies nicely into the natural slope of the land, an angle that makes it, and its clover-leaf bunker at front right, look scenic – even if the gradient from back to front makes it hell for some to two-putt. But that's all part of the fun, right?

info

The 11th
Par 3
207 metres

Formosa Golf Resort
110 Jack Lachlan Drive
Beachlands
Manukau
Tel (09) 536 5895
www.formosa.co.nz

The 16th at Formosa

MY FAVOURITE GOLF MOVIE is *The Greatest Game Ever Played*, the story of the 1913 United States Open that saw the greatest upset in the history of golf. It's a sports film that not only works, but is as good as the Mark Frost book on which it is based. Of other golf movies, *Caddyshack* is the funniest, *Happy Gilmore* the silliest, and *The Legend Of Bagger Vance* the best expression of what the 1920s German art critic Franz Roh called 'magic realism'.

Meanwhile, one of the worst is *Tin Cup*, a romantic comedy in which Kevin Costner plays a down and out pro, and Rene Russo his muse. The script is by Ron Shelton, who wrote one of the best sports movies of all time, *Bull Durham*, also starring Kevin Costner, but the only redeeming feature of *Tin Cup* is the music by the Texas Tornadoes.

Seeing *Tin Cup* reminded me of playing the par-5 16th hole at Formosa one day. There is a cathartic scene in the movie in which Costner, on the threshold of great success – about to win the girl *and* the money – overestimates his own ability and knocks the critical shot into water. Rather than lay up close to the hole, as any sensible player would, he then loses it: in a self-destructive rant, he repeats the same shot from the same spot, only to see his follow-up shots disappear into the water as well.

The 16th at Formosa is a long par 5 with a deep bush-clad gully and a stream cutting across the fairway in front of the green. The hole is

info

The 16th
Par 5
530 metres

Formosa Golf Resort
110 Jack Lachlan Drive
Beachlands
Manukau
Tel (09) 536 5895
www.formosa.co.nz

flanked by tall pines that frame the approach and act as a 'gateway' to the green, only the green is not straight over the stream, it is offset to the right.

That the green is offset makes even the longest hitters think twice about trying to reach it in two, or 'going for it'. Incidentally, this golf expression seems to be the domain of men only, rather like 'he's got balls'. Even the best female golfers, and they are legion, are not known for the power and length it takes to reach the green of a par 5 in two from the men's championship tees. So 'going for it' tends to be an exhortation for men… to try or accomplish, to achieve or fail, to look like champs or chumps in front of their golf buddies, one of whom is sure to be the lackey who has blurted out: 'Hey, he's going for it!'

Going for it on the 16th at Formosa is dangerous, even for men. Clearing the stream in two is not the issue as much as reaching a green tucked up and away to the right with two cloverleaf bunkers in front.

For male and female hacks, which means most of us, laying up is the best hope for scoring par. Yet even then the green is set back far enough that clearing the stream with a third shot cannot be taken for granted. It's a visual trick: the tall pine trees that frame the view make the green look closer than it really is. Which is why, after trying four times to clear the gully and reach the green, like Kevin Costner I said, '&@*$! it,' and moved on in silence to the 17th tee.

The 7th at The Grange

THE AIR NEW ZEALAND/SHELL OPEN was the second major professional golf tournament in New Zealand after the New Zealand Open. It was staged from 1975 to 1994, and often played at The Grange Golf Club. In 1992, at The Grange, it was won by Nick Price.

Price is a South African-born Zimbabwe citizen with English parents – such was the reach of Empire when he was born. When he played here he was thirty-five, had been a professional golfer for fifteen years, and was in the prime of his career.

That year he won the PGA Championship. Two years later he would win the British Open *and* the PGA Championship and become the top-ranked player in the world, a position he held for a year. In 2003, after a career total of forty-five wins worldwide, he was named to the World Golf Hall of Fame.

info

The 7th
Par 4
362 metres

The Grange Golf Club
2 Grange Road
Papatoetoe
Auckland
Tel (09) 278 9777
www.grangegolfclub.co.nz

Apart from his success on the course, the singular refrain associated with Nick Price was that he was 'one of the nicest guys in golf', as the television commentators liked to say over and over again.

Recently the 362-metre par-4 seventh hole at The Grange was closed while the club landscaped a small lake and made some other changes to the course. The 7th green was rebuilt, but it still plays the way it did during the 1992 Air New Zealand/Shell Open – as a short par 4 – but now over a deep gully to a two-tiered green.

Nick Price had a one-shot lead over Lucas Parsons when he came to the 7th. The pin was at the back of the green. Price struck the ball cleanly – so much so it bounced across the green past the pin, and shot through into the gallery. The ball might have continued on into ankle-high grass, perhaps forcing Price to drop a shot and even lose the tournament, had it not bounced off my shin.

This hurt slightly but I wasn't about to make a scene. If anything I felt embarrassed. I should have been paying attention, seen the ball coming, and moved out of the way. But I was standing two rows deep, behind a woman whose flowery wide-brimmed straw hat was blocking my view. I lost sight of the ball in the air and didn't see it bounce on the green… and then I felt it.

The ball rested on trampled grass, allowing Price to chip back close enough to the pin and save par. He eventually won the tournament by one stroke and ever since I've thought my shin played a part in that.

The 4th at Manukau

IN HIS BOOK *How to Play Golf*, published in 1912, the great Englishman Harry Vardon claimed there were two essentials to success in golf: the way you grip the club, and to what extent you are able to keep your head still when striking the ball.

Even though one of New Zealand's top coaches, Mal Tongue, has said he thinks the business about keeping the head still is a lot of bunkum, Vardon had to know what he was talking about: he had won six Open Championships, a record that still stands.

Vardon was the greatest player of his era – call it *fin de siècle* – and we know him even better today, thanks to *The Greatest Game Ever Played* by Mark Frost, a book many believe to be the best on golf ever written. It tells the story of the 1913 United States Open, where Vardon, the world's number one player and hands-down favourite to win, lost to Francis Ouimet, a young amateur who was best known as one of the caddies at the club where the tournament was played.

You can argue about keeping the head still or not, but no one disputes that Vardon was spot-on when it came to teaching someone how to grip a golf club – so much so that the most popular grip used in golf today is named for him: the Vardon grip.

It's not my business here to explain the Vardon grip – see your nearest PGA pro for that – but if you do not learn the Vardon grip properly, and practise it, there is a very good chance your tee shot on the par-4

fourth hole at the Manukau Golf Club could wind up in the Manukau Harbour.

In 1998, the Dunedin touring pro Greg Turner reshaped four holes at Manukau, including the 4th. At only 250 metres long from the back tee, it is certainly one of the shortest par 4s in New Zealand. But because Turner placed the tees back and brought more of the harbour into play, it takes little more than the wrong grip to turn the club face and send the ball sailing left into the drink. Play here when the tide is out and you may be able to retrieve the ball, albeit with mud on your shoes.

Of course, if you *want* to hook a ball into the harbour for fun, be my guest. Vijay Singh did it all the time for practice when he lived near here many years ago.

info

The 4th
Par 4
250 metres

Manukau Golf Club
1 Great South Road
Takanini
Tel (09) 266 8297
www.manukaugolf.co.nz

The 12th at Clarks Beach

ONE OF MY FAVOURITE GOLF HOLES, the second at Muriwai, no longer exists. Stormy seas ate away that black-sand coast, taking the second green with it. The hole was a short par 3 but it played straight into the teeth of the westerly. On windy days it was great fun trying to drive the ball with a driver to a green just 120 metres away.

Muriwai has since been rebuilt in response to the loss of coastline, so if mad-dog golfers want to test themselves against such elements now they have to play the 12th hole at the Clarks Beach Golf Club.

Manukau Harbour, the second largest harbour in New Zealand after the Kaipara, acts for golfers more like the sea than a harbour because it is big and open and exposed. The 12th backs up to the harbour, and there are no trees behind the green to act as a wind break.

There is a photo of the hole on the scorecard, so you can get an idea of what you're in for before you get there, but as you would expect the photo was taken on a calm sunny day. Fine days do occur and they make Clarks Beach one of the country's true hidden gems, but what fun is a fine day?

info

The 12th
Par 3
130 metres

Clarks Beach Golf Club
100 Stevenson Road
Clarks Beach
Tel (09) 232 1788
www.clarksbeachgolfclub.co.nz

The 4th at Pukekohe

FOR ALL THE WELL-KNOWN GOLF COURSE DESIGNERS who have had, and are having, a major impact on the look of golf in New Zealand – for example, Jack Nicklaus, Tom Doak, Bob Charles and Greg Turner – the greatest change in recent years has arguably been inspired by a little known family team from Canada. Based in Edmonton, Sid Puddicombe and his three sons, Grant, Mark, and Tod, are Puddicombe Golf, whose speciality is as much golf hole reconstruction as it is designing and building an entirely new course.

Most of their work is in Alberta, but Puddicombe Golf has worked on alterations and complete 18-hole designs in the United States, Japan and New Zealand. The company designed the entire 18-hole layout at Lakes Resort in Pauanui, while at six other courses around the country their work has involved reshaping a hole or series of holes.

Puddicombe Golf's website claims their aim is to build player-friendly holes, but their record in New Zealand has been to create holes that, while wonderful to look at, are not at all player-friendly – if there is even such a thing.

Puddicombe did a splendid job on the 4th at Pukekohe Golf Club. The par-3 hole plays over a new pond installed by the team in 2004. It is 160 metres long from the back tee, and calls for a carry over water to a two-tiered green that slopes away in all directions from the middle. A large bunker on the left catches those who try too hard.

The improvement to this hole is an example of how a course can look better and be more environmentally sensible. Let's face it, no one wants to see their tee shot splash down somewhere, anywhere, yet a water hazard is an aesthetic addition in a way a sand trap is not. Add a pond at the right place and it can change a golf hole from a pauper to a prince. And here the pond and its charming fountain also serve as a sustainable source of irrigation.

info

The 4th
Par 3
160 metres

Pukekohe Golf Club
State Highway 22
Pukekohe
Tel (09) 294 8822
www.pukekohegolf.co.nz

The 8th at Thames

UNTIL SHE PASSED AWAY in April 2008 at the age of ninety-seven, Clarice Espiner was a life member of the Thames Golf Club. She was still playing regularly, either in the club's 9-hole event on Wednesdays or the usual 18-hole round on Saturday mornings, right up until a month before she died.

As the club manager, Don Warner, told me, 'She had her own motorised golf cart but it was still a feat at her age to play our course, which is advertised as being on "undulating terrain" – in other words, pretty bloody hilly.'

Perhaps no other hole represents the changing nature of the course at Thames more than the par-3 eighth, known for obvious reasons as 'The Drop'. It plays from an extremely elevated tee down to the green about 130 metres away. Seniors, if they choose to use it, have their own tee at the bottom of the hill just 85 metres from the hole.

Let me brutally frank: most weekend golfers cannot even hit a green from 85 metres, much less get close to the hole. We are even less likely to score a hole-in-one, which is what Clarice Espiner did in 2004 at the age of ninety-four. I'm willing to venture a guess that made Clarice the oldest person in New Zealand ever to score a hole-in-one.

Clarice, who still drove a car, would play golf then go home and mow the lawn, for she was a keen gardener and she liked things tidy. Take the

time, while you're playing at Thames, to pull a weed or two from the flower beds between the 11th and 17th tees. Clarice kept a garden here for many years, and it is known officially as Clarice Espiner Corner.

Clarice once told a journalist for the *Listener* that she attributed her longevity to good genes, a good diet and a positive attitude. But all that golf must surely have played a part.

info

The 8th
Par 3
130 metres

Thames Golf Club
State Highway 26
Kirikiri, Thames
Tel (07) 868 9062
www.thames.nzgolf.net

The 17th at Lakes Resort

THE AVERAGE PLAYER does not swing at the ball so much as chop at it, thus he or she can be called a 'hack'. I believe I speak for all hacks when I say that for a variety of reasons, from not practising to body type to mental attitude, the fundamental problem with our game is that we have never developed a fluid, muscular, coordinated swing.

Professionals and the best amateurs *swing* a golf club. Watching them hit a golf ball is like watching a fine performance, a dancer perhaps, where no movement is uncertain or shaky. Every move is smooooooth.

Watching a hack, on the other hand, is like watching someone drowning. Short par 3s frustrate the hell out of us because we have little or no ability to control our distance, even with 'short irons', while par-4 holes are often too long and too narrow and have too many goddamn trees. That is why, for most of us, one of the best opportunities we have

of scoring par is a short par 5 with a wide fairway.

For hacks, such holes are like walking from a noisy street into a cathedral. All is calm, quiet and relaxed, and we surprise ourselves and everyone else by striking the ball pure and straight, reaching the green in the regulation three, and two-putting for par. On the best days we putt for a birdie from twenty feet.

info

The 17th
Par 5
405 metres

Lakes Resort
100 Augusta Drive
Pauanui
Tel (07) 864 5106
www.lakesresort.com

The par-5 seventeenth at Lakes Resort, Pauanui, on the Coromandel Peninsula, is 405 metres long so it is perfect for hacks – and the journey along the way is utterly unique for the landscaping of the fairway and the green, the placement of bunkers, and the seemingly innocuous stream that cuts across the fairway just in front of the green.

The hole calls for thoughtful club selection, in order to place the ball in a certain spot off the tee, in order to set up the best possible approach to the green. Hacks generally do not like target golf, but this is one short par 5 not to be missed, even if the fairway is not as wide as it should be.

The 17th at Omokoroa

THE BAR-TAILED GODWIT (*Limosa lapponica baueri*) is one of four species of godwit, and the only one that flies annually non-stop from Alaska to New Zealand. Talk about long-haul travel. The birds breed on the Arctic coast in the northern hemisphere summer, and before they fly to New Zealand they fill their bellies to maximum capacity. The 11,000-kilometre journey, during which they do not feed at all, is believed to be an ornithological record.

The trip takes about ten days. The birds arrive in New Zealand in September looking pretty ragged, as you might expect, but they recover quickly thanks to peace and quiet and plenty of edible creatures on the shore of Tauranga Harbour and other tidal flats up and down the Bay of Plenty. On top of this, around a thousand non-breeding godwits don't go to Alaska, but stay in the harbour for the winter.

So take care when you play the 17th hole at Omokoroa (also known as Western Bays Golf Links) just west of Tauranga. The course is known as much for its famous birds as it is for golf: a dove stops by for a visit and sits around inside the clubhouse, ducks are constantly waddling in to see what's up, but the star of the birds is the bar-tailed godwit. The 17th is a par 3 that plays directly toward the harbour, and its green is close to the water's edge, the very place where you may find godwits wading about, poking their beaks into tidal mud for a feed.

At 140 metres from the yellow tee, the nearest one, this hole is a dangerous distance for the godwit: it requires a mid to long iron and shot, which can just as easily wind up on the beach as the green.

While you're there, have a look out for these other species known to frequent the neighbourhood: the white-faced heron, Australasian pied stilt, South Island pied oystercatcher, Hudsonian godwit, Asiatic black-tailed godwit and Caspian tern. No matter what sort of round you play, the bird-watching will be a bonus.

info

The 17th
Par 3
140 metres

Omokoroa Golf Club
Links View Drive
Tauranga
Tel (07) 548 0384
www.omokoroagolf.co.nz

The 12th at Tauranga

KELVIN DAVID GEORGE NAGLE, commonly known as Kel, was 39 when he won the British Open in 1960. Had you placed a bet on Nagle to win that tournament you would have won a lot of money because the overall favourite and popular choice was Arnold Palmer. Palmer had won the Masters earlier that year, and now that television was bringing golf to the world for the first time The King, as he was known, had quickly become one of the most famous names in sport.

Unless you lived in New Zealand or Australia, not even the most ardent golf fans knew who Kel Nagle was, even though he had won two World Cups of Golf for Australia, playing with British Open winner Peter Thomson in 1954 and 1959. Television coverage of golf had yet to extend down under.

Nagle's victory at St Andrews was a huge upset, not only because he was an unknown but because he had had to par the last two holes to beat Arnold Palmer by one shot.

Nagle won just that one Major, and he was the United States Open runner-up in 1965, but outside of that his fame lies in his incredible sixty-one Australasian Tour wins – fifteen of them in New Zealand. In the 1960s and '70s he won the New Zealand Open seven times and the NZ PGA championship eight times. Accordingly, in the Bay of Plenty, where he played many times, he was a popular figure.

The Tauranga Golf Club is situated next to a racetrack, and no doubt there have been moments when an owner thought he might lose his stud horse to a stray drive, particularly on the par-5 thirteenth, where a track fence marks out of bounds.

The 12th
Par 3
120 metres

info

Tauranga Golf Club
Cameron Road
Tauranga
Tel (07) 578 8465
www.taurangagolf.co.nz

The club's signature hole, however, is the par-3 twelfth, 'The Knell'. This hole is only about 120 metres long, but it plays out to an extremely elevated green. As if the steep drop-off were not enough, there is a sand trap directly in front of the green.

When Kel Nagle once teed up here, his shot fell short and bounced away into the rough. It took him five shots to finally stop the ball on the green, from where he two-putted for a seven. Yet as angry and embarrassed as the great Australian pro must have felt in front of a large gallery of fans, spare a thought for the late Betty Johnson, who set the club record here with a 37.

The 18th at Mount Maunganui

THE FIVE COURSE CLASSIC claims to be the largest individual Stableford tournament in the world. For the uninitiated, a Stableford tournament is decided not on the fewest strokes, but on an accumulation of points, where the number of points earned on any given hole depends on the player's handicap. The system was invented by a doctor called Frank Stableford, who apparently drove a yellow Rolls-Royce and wore a polka-dot bow tie. He later recalled: 'I was practising on the second fairway at Wallasey Golf Club one day in the latter part of 1931, when the thought ran through my mind that many players in competitions got very little fun since they tore up their cards after playing only a few holes, and I wondered if anything could be done about it.' For non-stroke play tournaments, Stableford is a popular format because it gives even high handicappers an equal chance of winning on the day.

The Five Course Classic takes place in the Bay of Plenty every February. The 90-hole event attracts nearly 500 starters, and is played over five days on five different courses: Tauranga, Omokoroa, Omanu, Te Puke and Mount Maunganui.

It's easy to imagine someone standing on the 18th green at Mount Maunganui, after having played 89 holes of the Five Course Classic, having a nerve-wrecking putt for the points needed to win.

The 18th is a par 4, 339 metres long from the tips. It's one of the loveliest closing holes in New Zealand golf, shaped as it is by ancient

sand dunes – the course is only a long iron from the beach – and framed by pohutukawa trees, the clubhouse and, beyond that, the tip of the mountain itself.

When the history of the NZ PGA championship is written, it may include a story of a putt needed at this hole for a win: that tournament, equal in status to the New Zealand Open, was held here for many years. A generation of New Zealand stars, who went on to have success overseas, had memorable victories. Bob Charles and John Lister each won the NZ PGA three times, Frank Nobilo twice, and Simon Owen and Greg Turner once each. The 18th hole at the Mount is permeated with moments both personal and historical.

info

The 18th
Par 4
339 metres

Mount Maunganui Golf Club
15 Fairway Avenue
Mount Maunganui
Tel (07) 572 7044
www.mountgolf.co.nz

The 6th at Te Puke

TE PUKE CALLS ITSELF the Kiwifruit Capital of the World. There's probably an Italian grower somewhere near Emilia-Romagna scoffing at that, because Italy now produces more kiwifruit than New Zealand. Still, ninety percent of the millions of trays of kiwifruit that New Zealand exports each year comes from Te Puke. Next time you're driving through the town, a visit to an exhibition called Kiwi360 will leave you knowing more about kiwifruit than the average Italian.

Bay of Plenty kiwifruit growers have Isabel Fraser to thank for their success. In 1904 Fraser, the principal of Wanganui Girls College, visited her sister's mission station in China and brought back seeds of *yang tao*. She gave the seeds to an orchardist, who had them planted, and three years later they bore fruit, damn fine fruit, better even than those Fraser had tasted in Asia. In 1939 a horticulturalist put in some plants in Te Puke and a new industry was born. Back then the fruit were known as Chinese gooseberries; they were christened 'kiwifruit' in 1959.

The world price of kiwifruit has dropped in recent years but the industry is still a big deal in Te Puke, and to get a first-hand impression all you need to do is play golf. The Te Puke Golf Club, one of the nicest country courses in the North Island, borders a large kiwifruit orchard.

The 6th hole here, a 322-metre par 4, is the No. 1 stroke hole on the course. The orchard that runs down the right-hand side of the fairway is out of bounds, of course. What grower in his or her right mind

would want golfers knocking balls into their orchard? But it is not the orchard, and the threat of out of bounds, that makes this hole so formidable. It is the trees that branch way out into the fairway on the left, a fairway that slopes left to right where the prevailing wind is left to right. Score par here and you deserve a complimentary kiwifruit pavlova.

info

The 6th
Par 4
322 metres

Te Puke Golf Club
847 State Highway Two
Te Puke
Tel (07) 533 1115
www.tepukegolf.co.nz

The 13th at Whakatane

LIKE A LOT OF GOLF CLUBS TODAY, the Whakatane Golf Club issues a scorecard designed to be tallied by a computer, not a human being. There is good reason for this: a computerised scorecard can be processed faster – assuming the player has marked it right, which means striking a mark across a number from 1 to 10 for a score at a hole that no longer has a name.

If the thirteenth hole at Whakatane had a name it might be 'Mary's Garden', and there's a sign close to the tee announcing as much. This is where the late Mary Good and her friends kept a flower garden. It's the only personalised garden on the course, although it's small and might not be appreciated by a guest if not for the sign. Some of Mary's family still play here, and friends still look after her garden.

The hole might also be called 'George's Triumph' or 'Jackson's Revenge'. It was at this par-5 hole many years ago that a Scotsman and club member George Jackson scored a two, known in the game as an albatross or double eagle – a remarkable feat that may never happen here again, even with recent changes in club and ball technology.

Another albatross is unlikely because the hole has a sharp dog-leg right, with a spine running up the middle of the fairway, a feature that recalls the movie *Alien*. The dog-leg and the shape of the fairway make the hole decidedly strategic. The fairway slopes severely from right to left, and the left side of the fairway sits below the green. How George

Jackson managed to get the ball up and rolling, straight on to the green and then *in the hole* … for a two … is hard to imagine. It must be one of the great feats of New Zealand golf, even if it's unknown outside the Bay of Plenty.

Unlike Mary Good, George was a cantankerous old soul who, by virtue of his Scottish heritage, felt he was more in tune with the gods of the game than others. In the end he wasn't especially popular among members. That may explain why the sign identifying Mary's garden is a lot bigger than the small memorial to George on a bench.

info

The 13th
Par 5
497 metres

Whakatane Golf Club
Golf Links Road
Whakatane
Tel (07) 308 8117
www.whakatanegolf.com

The 14th at Ohope

THE NEW ZEALAND DOTTEREL – tuturiwhatu pukunui in Maori, *Charadrius obscurus* in Latin – is close to extinction. These endemic shorebirds have been reduced to a population of less than two thousand because of shoreline developments such as the one at Ohope Beach.

A sandy spit at Ohiwa Harbour in the Bay of Plenty, Ohope Beach has housing and a neat links golf course along the shore, but the council was wise enough to preserve some land for the dotterel. If the birds could talk, my guess is they would say they are as unhappy about the golf course as about the housing development. So please, try not to make life even more difficult for these endangered creatures by disrespecting their sanctuary. It's all around you as you play here, but foremost you'll see it from the 14th green.

The 14th hole at the Ohope Golf Club is a par 5 that plays directly out towards the end of the spit and the dedicated dotterel sanctuary. To say this wonderful par 5 plays straight, however, is to misrepresent the idiosyncratic nature of the hole – aside from the birds.

Ask regulars here which is the signature hole and most will tell you the 4th, if only because the tee is the highest point on the course, the observation platform for the best sea view. Or they may volunteer the 5th hole, because it plays over the clubhouse road; before teeing off, players are asked to switch on a red light as a warning to cars coming and going.

But really the finest hole on this modest but visually strong links, a hole that would not be out of place on the great Scottish links courses, is the 14th: it is scenic, has a new oversized two-tier green, and at 480 metres from the white tee is not unduly long for the average player. On a fine day this is as good as golf gets, but please do not go looking for lost balls in the bird sanctuary, and do leave your dog at home.

info

The 14th
Par 5
480 metres

Ohope International Golf Club
Harbour Road
Ohope
Tel (07) 312 4486
www.ohope.nzgolf.net

The 16th at Springfield

DANNY LEE'S IS A REMARKABLE STORY. On August 24, 2008, the eighteen-year-old became the youngest player ever to win the men's US Amateur – a championship that has run for 113 years. Lee broke the record set by Tiger Woods, who was six months older than Lee when he won his first US Amateur. Naturally, this touched off a rash of speculation under the banner: 'The Next Tiger Woods?' Let's hope so.

Lee's story has an added twist: when he was eleven years old his parents, both golfers – his mother a professional – made the extraordinary decision to leave their homeland of South Korea to improve the chances for their young son to succeed in golf, and they chose New Zealand as the place to do that.

And why not? As the Lees learned one summer during a preliminary visit, New Zealand has a wealth of golf courses – and seemingly no one playing them. Of course that's not true, but if you're accustomed to the Dong Seoul Country Club, which, like all golf clubs in Asia, is overcrowded with people there as much for the swimming pool, tennis courts and good food as for golf, the Springfield Golf Club in Rotorua, New Zealand must have looked like some kind of paradise. Added to that was the fact the local boys high school had a highly respected golf academy.

The Lees settled in Rotorua, joined Springfield and before long their prodigy son had set the course record by shooting a sizzling 62 in the

inaugural 2007 Springfield Open. And after becoming the best amateur player in New Zealand, he then became number one in the world at Pinehurst, North Carolina. One week later, he proudly became a New Zealand citizen.

It's a great story, and although Brenda Ormsby, one of New Zealand's top women professionals, and the club pro at Springfield, told me that as far as she knew Lee hadn't yet scored a hole-in-one at the 16th, it probably won't be long before he does.

The 16th at Springfield is one of the finest par 3s in the Bay of Plenty. Why? Because it is straightforward, even simple, and sometimes the best golf holes, like the best recipes, are simple. It is 192 metres long from the back tee, but its wide-mouth green is balanced neatly by sand traps on the sides and framed by a mix of native trees out the back.

info

The 16th
Par 3
192 metres

Springfield Golf Club
Devon Street West
Rotorua
Tel (07) 348 9723
www.springfieldgolf.co.nz

The 14th at Arikikapakapa

IT MIGHT BE THOUGHT that golf tourism in New Zealand began in 1970 with the opening of Wairakei International Golf Course by the government's Tourist Hotel Corporation. In fact, the idea of using golf to attract tourists to New Zealand dates back to 1902, when a government decree declared that golf links 'would provide a source of pleasure to many visitors'.

The Rotorua Golf Club was established in 1906, and in 1912, after a couple of false starts, it settled on its current site on Arikikapakapa Reserve, land that had been gifted to the Crown by Ngati Whakaue.

Arikikapakapa means the plopping noise made by hot mud from thermal activity in the area. It is also the name of a mythical paramount Maori chief who arrived in Aotearoa only to find it too wet and cold in winter. He asked a sister in Hawaiki to send fire to keep him warm, thus bringing about the thermal activity that lies beneath the site of today's golf course.

The course was reworked in 1996 and the result is at least one must-play hole, if not two. The par-3 ninth might be considered essential because it is the only golf hole in New Zealand that has ever been featured on a postage stamp. Maybe the aim was to romanticise the idea of playing golf in sulphuric air, with steam vents for hazards.

But in my opinion the par-3 fourteenth is even more expressive: not only does it have thermal activity, it also plays across Lake Arikikapakapa

to a green that slopes left to right towards two lovely new sand traps. From the back tee the hole is 186 metres long, which is to say from that distance on any given day as many balls wind up in bubbling mud or in the lake as on the green. And do watch out for the thermal crater – descent is not advised!

info

The 14th
Par 3
186 metres

Rotorua Golf Club
399 Fenton Street
Rotorua
Tel (07) 348 4051
www.rotoruagolfclub.co.nz

39

The 1st at Horsham Downs

WHEN THIS SWEET LITTLE NINE-HOLE COURSE north of the Hamilton CBD on River Road opened in 1945, Geoff McNally was one of the prime movers and shakers among the founding members, so it was appropriate that he be named the first club captain and have the honour of hitting the first ball.

People gathered around, and as it was 1945 they certainly had plenty to cheer about: the end of the war was in sight. McNally gave them something more to cheer about, and, like the war, it was something they would remember for the rest of their lives.

The opening hole here is a par 3 and about 160 metres long. There is a bunker on the right, and the two-tiered green slopes a little from left to right. McNally accepted the handshake and a new Dunlop 7 ball from the newly elected club president. He took a 5-iron from his bag, teed the ball up, squared off, and without blinking an eye brought the club back and through the ball, making a solid strike.

The ball had plenty of loft, that's the first thing people noticed, and the closer it got to the green the more apparent it was that it was heading straight for the flag, a brand new flag on a virgin green. New club, new ball, new flag, new green, first official shot… The ball bounced once or twice before disappearing into the hole.

Needless to say, that shot was the talk of the Waikato for years to

come. To my surprise – it was a long time ago after all – I reached Geoff McNally by telephone; he confirmed the story and added: 'I did it again on closing day.'

'You made another hole-in-one at the first?' I said.

'No, the second one was at the third.'

They were, McNally said, the only two holes-in-one he has ever had.

info

The 1st
Par 3
160 metres

Horsham Downs Golf Club
1991 River Road
Hamilton
Tel (07) 829 4709
www.horshamdownsgolf.co.nz

The 18th at St Andrews

THE ST ANDREWS COURSE of the Hamilton Golf Club has played host to five New Zealand Opens and six New Zealand Amateur Championships, and produced a host of talented professionals such as Jan Arnold, Steve Alker and David Smail, so great stories emanate from the bar.

Among the best concern goings-on at the 18th hole, a par 3 with a famous bunker stretching across its front like a bandana around the neck – one that chokes you if you tie it too tight.

The 18th
Par 3
136 metres

info

Hamilton Golf Club
64 St Andrews Terrace
Hamilton
Tel (07) 849 2069
www.standrews.co.nz

In 1958 Peter Thomson, winner of five Open Championships, birdied this 18th to get second place at the New Zealand Open by a single shot over a little known golf prodigy from South Africa named Gary Player. Player, then twenty-two, would go on to win nine major championships, including the British Open three times – 1959, 1968 and 1974. Thomson would win the Open five times, but no other Majors. Meanwhile Kel Nagle, who beat them both that day at St Andrews, would win only one Major, the Open in 1960.

The 18th is only 136 metres long from the back tees, so it tends to be little or no problem for pros. But the bunker, and the fact that the green sits up where only a full carry will get the job done, means that it wreaks havoc on the play of amateurs. Most of us haven't a clue how to play a shot out of a sand trap. Most of us have never even taken the time to think about it. A shallow trap here or a deep trap there, it makes no difference: in sand we are hopelessly lost.

So it was on the day that two club members each knocked their ball into the trap in front of the 18th green. One of them had a bit of trouble getting out; he took fifteen strokes to get the ball on to the green. And when he did, he discovered he had played the wrong ball.

The rule for playing the wrong ball out of a hazard is this: 'If a player plays any strokes in a hazard with the wrong ball there is no penalty.' In this instance, the ball was returned to the bunker. The player then played what was rightfully his ball, and this time he got it out and on to the green in one and made his putt for par.

The 18th at Narrows

THE WAIKATO RIVER rises in the snow and ice of Tongariro National Park. At 425 kilometres it is the country's longest river, and so swift in places that crossing it any way other than using a bridge is unthinkable. Dip your toe in at your peril.

There is a spot, however, where the water is low and slow, and where Tainui Maori often forged a crossing. The narrowest part of the river, it can be found at Tamahere, down the airport road off State Highway One south of Hamilton, just below Narrows Golf Club.

The club is named for that place in the river – not, as the joke goes, for its narrow fairways, although this would be appropriate: some of the fairways here are so narrow you have to hit the ball straight or die. Yes, I'm exaggerating … a little.

When he finally retires from the professional tours, David Smail will undoubtedly be described in the media as a Waikato golf legend. Born in Hamilton, he has won five times on the Japan tour, and in 2001 he won the New Zealand Open. Yet one of the proudest moments of his entire career may have happened in February 2008 at the 18th hole of Narrows.

The 18th is a short par 3, only 114 metres long from the tips. But it's scary because it plays from an elevated tee to a plateau green, where the hazard is not so much the bunker on the left as all the faces of people watching from the clubhouse lounge.

The 18th green and the big picture window of the clubhouse are made for each other, and there was a full gallery looking on when David Smail stepped to the tee that day – more than the usual weekend gathering, because it was a charity event. This is what great players have to put up with on a golf course: they can't blow their nose without a lot of people watching.

Smail was there more as a father than a pro golfer: he was doing his bit in a fund-raising event for Tamahere School. He had not played the course in twenty years, and since his time in New Zealand is a holiday one of the last things he probably wanted to do was pick up a golf club.

With a slight breeze in his face, he set up over the ball with a pitching wedge in his hands. The shot sailed high and straight, landed on the green behind the pin and spun back, straight into the cup.

info

The 18th
Par 3
114 metres

Narrows Golf Club
Airport Road
Hamilton
Tel (07) 856 5207
www.nzgolfcourses.co.nz/narrows

The 4th at Cambridge

IT HAD BEEN A VERY BAD DAY for Reti Keenar: in a Saturday club scramble, he had had to play the back nine first. That's the problem with scrambles, they can scramble the brain too. Keenar triple-bogeyed the 10th, then double-bogeyed the 11th, then broke his driver.

Keenar was on a 13 handicap, so it's easy to imagine him whacking the driver against the ground in anger at being five over par after two holes. Whatever, he played on, using a borrowed driver.

Reti Keenar's group was playing from the white tees. The 4th hole at the Cambridge Golf Club is 320 metres long from this tee. The hole is a dog-leg left, and because there is a row of trees down the left side of the fairway the conventional approach is to simply follow the fairway around. Big hitters with low handicaps, and young pros such as Cambridge's James Gill – who in 2008 joined Danny Lee on the United States amateur circuit – might show off and go left over the trees for a direct shot at the green. But for most of us that would be about as possible as winning the New Zealand Open.

Keenar's game settled down. His group had completed the back nine and were making their way around the front when he stepped up to the tee at the 4th. 'I just hit it,' he would later tell a reporter from *The Waikato Times*.

The ball disappeared left over the trees. After taking time to look for it under the trees – who knew, maybe it had ricocheted off a branch –

Keenar played a second ball. On the green, he was the first to putt out. He was being asked if he wanted the pin in or out when someone saw a ball lying at the bottom of the cup. Reti Keenar had scored a hole-in-one on a par 4.

But golf can be cruel. Because he had already played out with a second ball, the score of his first ball did not count.

info

The 4th
Par 4
320 metres

Cambridge Golf Club
State Highway One
Cambridge
Tel (07) 827 6381
www.cambridgegolf.co.nz

The 6th at Waitomo

'MY FIRST GOLF EXPERIENCE was caddying for my dad when I was seven years old at the Waitomo Golf Club,' Phil Tataurangi says on his website.

Tataurangi went on to become one of New Zealand's most accomplished professionals. At the 1992 Eisenhower Trophy, the world amateur team championship for men, he was the best individual player, and – with Michael Campbell, Grant Moorehead and Stephen Scahill – one of the foursome who won the team trophy.

After he turned professional the following year, he won twice on the Nike (now Nationwide) Tour, won the Australian PGA Championship, and in 2002 the Invensys Classic in Las Vegas – his only win on the United States PGA Tour. But by then his golf swing had messed with his body to the point where a serious lower back injury was forcing him from the game altogether.

Tataurangi's earliest days playing golf at Waitomo were spent with a threesome known famously as 'the old ladies'. More than anyone, Tataurangi credits Waitomo Golf Club members Jessie Snowden, Zina Quinn and Darl Hetet with teaching him the rules, the etiquette, and how to have fun playing – even off a 32 handicap.

The 6th at Waitomo, generally acknowledged as the club's signature hole, features Wilma Butcher's nicely planted garden on the left, a placid little pond between the tee and the green (leave the goldfish

alone, please), and a green that slopes right to left towards a bunker. I suspect the hole, as lovely a par 3 as it is, never caused Tataurangi any trouble. It is only 149 metres long from the back tee, and with the help and guidance of 'the old ladies' he was still just eleven years old when he won the senior men's club title at Puahue Golf Club in Te Awamutu.

The ground to the left of the 6th green used to be a swamp – and then Mack Waretini senior, a former member of the 28th Maori Battalion, retired. With nothing much to do, Mack spent a year or so fiddling about with little more than a shovel and a wheelbarrow, hauling dirt and filling it in. That's why today it's called Mack's Walk.

info

The 6th
Par 3
149 metres

Waitomo Golf Club
68 Golf Road
Otorohanga
Tel (07) 873 7125
www.waitomo.nzgolf.net

The 14th at Poverty Bay

TE UPOKO O TE KURI A PAOA, roughly translated, means 'the head of the dog of Paoa'. According to local tradition, Paoa, a Maori chief, commanded *Horouta*, a canoe that arrived in Poverty Bay from Hawaiki many centuries ago.

Today, Te Upoko o Te Kuri a Paoa is better known as Young Nick's Head. This stunning clifftop peninsula, which shapes the lower end of Poverty Bay, was named for Nicholas Young, the cabin boy on Captain James Cook's ship *Endeavour* who, on October 6, 1769, was the first person on board to spy New Zealand.

In 2002 local Maori, Ngai Tamanuhiri, protested when the land, part of a large sheep station, was to be sold to a New York financier. In response, the government bought the cliffs, pa site and peak and gifted them into public ownership, and the New Yorker agreed to protect the cultural and historical values of the property.

Young Nick's Head forms a unique backdrop to the 14th hole at the Poverty Bay Golf Club, also known as Awapuni Links. If this fine golf course were located close to a major city, the demand for tee times would mean booking well in advance. As it is, on this under-populated coast it is possible to roll up and play almost any time, any day of the week.

The 14th is a par 4, 314 metres long from the back tee. It plays over dunes along the outer edge of the course; a fence line marks out of bounds on one side of the fairway.

John Rouse, an avid golfer with an interest in local history – he has written *Links with the Past*, a history of golf in Poverty Bay – says the land on which this hole is sited was commandeered in the Second World War by the Royal New Zealand Air Force because of its proximity to the Gisborne airport, then called Darton Field. The RNZAF station at Gisborne was responsible for daily reconnaissance patrols from Cape Kidnappers to East Cape and out over the Pacific during the years 1942 to 1945.

info

The 14th
Par 4
314 metres

Poverty Bay Golf Club
Lytton Road
Gisborne
Tel (06) 867 4402
www.gisbornegolf.co.nz

The greens here are among the best in the country, thanks to the foresight of the club, which had them planted in the 1970s with a durable and attractive strain of grass known as Penncross bentgrass. If you're thinking golf, imagine a nicely cut 14th green on a summer's day with Young Nick's Head as a dramatic backdrop, changing colour throughout the day.

The 16th at Maraenui

NAPIER IN HAWKE'S BAY is known for two related things: the 7.8 magnitude earthquake that devastated the city in 1931, and the art deco buildings that sprung from the ruins and today attract architecture aficionados from around the world.

In 1955, in a less momentous event, fire gutted the clubhouse of the Maraenui Golf Club, which lies a stone's throw from the city's centre. Afterwards, beneath a trapdoor where the bar had been, someone discovered an unharmed case of Bell's Whisky. Ever since – or since 1959 to be exact – the club has staged an annual Bell's Whisky tournament, a competition that is, as you might guess, more social than serious.

To what extent the legendary South African champion Gary Player had anything to do with the tournament's creation is not known. Probably nothing at all. But Player did play here the year before in an exhibition match with fellow South African Harold Henning and Australian Peter Thomson. In the following decade he won nine majors, his first the Open Championship in 1959. Who knows, maybe he celebrated this British Open victory with a Bell's.

The 16th at Maraenui is a 188-metre par 3 from the back tee, and as a golf hole it could not be more straightforward. Its large circular green is slightly elevated with roll back off the front, and there is a bunker nearby, but what distinguishes it are the three giant Phoenix palms at the back, positioned like Aussie Rules goalposts – and the fact that on

this hole in 1958 Harold Henning upstaged Gary Player by scoring a birdie, and then set a course record of 64.

That record is shared today with Stuart Duff of the Hastings Golf Club. Duff shot a sizzling 64 here too… only wait just a minute. Duff shot his 64 (*eight* under par) on a course that was par 72. Henning shot his 64 when the course was par 73. Does that mean that Henning's nine-under round (with the birdie at the 16th) is actually a 63 on the current layout, and that he alone holds the course record? Or have I been drinking too much whisky?

info

The 16th
Par 3
188 metres

Maraenui Golf Club
Te Awa Avenue
Napier
Tel (06) 835 8656
www.maraenuigolf.co.nz

The 16th at Waiohiki

WHEN LAND FROM the McLean family was combined with Maori leasehold land to make up a full eighteen holes for the Napier Golf Club's Waiohiki Links in 1896, one of the club's ardent enthusiasts was Kurupo Tareha. Tareha was the son of a principal chief of Ngati Kahungunu. He had developed an interest in golf after being taken to St Andrews in Scotland during a visit to Britain for Queen Victoria's sixtieth birthday.

Tareha's portrait hangs in the clubhouse today, and rightly so, for in 1903 he won the first New Zealand amateur golf championship.

As fathers do, Tareha introduced his son Kapi to golf. And as sons do, Kapi soon outshone his father, establishing a reputation as one of the longest hitters of a golf ball in Hawke's Bay. Kapi is said to have been famous for driving the par-4 eighteenth green – and that was in the days when balls were made of feathers.

Kapi not only won golf championships around the lower half of the North Island, he won cups for many other sports as well, including rugby, boxing and athletics. He was the Bay's greatest athlete, and a memorial carving close to the 9th hole is dedicated to him.

Kapi's daughter Audrey (later Audrey Mullany) became, in turn, one of the greatest women golfers in the province, winning the club championship many times, the Hawke's Bay Open twice, and the New Zealand Maori Golf Association's national title many times.

The 16th
Par 4
384 metres

info

Napier Golf Club
1215 State Highway 50
Napier
Tel (06) 844 7913
www.napiergolf.co.nz

The original ownership of the land by the Tareha whanau has an interesting grace note on the course: the 16th hole may be the only golf hole in New Zealand that abuts grave sites, which are chained off near the green. Out of respect for the dead, a club rule states that a ball may be lifted without penalty if it lies within two club lengths of the graves.

The question is: Who is buried here? Because the site is on the original Tereha land, it is generally agreed that the graves, which are of two young girls, belong to members of that family. The cause of their deaths is unknown, although one local historian has speculated that they died in the infamous 1918 influenza epidemic.

The 16th is a long par 4, 384 metres from the blue tees. It plays around to the left slightly, favouring players who can draw the ball, but whether you draw the ball or not is not as critical as finding the green, not the grave site, with your second shot.

The 6th at Cape Kidnappers

TOM DOAK, the author of a number of books on golf course design, studied landscape architecture because, from a young age, golf course design was the profession he wanted to pursue. Many American students complete their degrees and head off to Europe to see the usual sights and be wild and crazy, before heading back home to take up the challenges of the real world. Tom Doak went to Europe too, but he went to study golf courses, namely the Old Course at St Andrews, where he spent a summer working as a caddy and getting to know every nook and cranny.

Doak worked with the great American designer Pete Dye before setting out on his own. Today he is one of the most sought after designers in the world, and one of his gems is Cape Kidnappers, a course that expresses everything about an approach he's developed since that impressionable summer in Scotland.

He calls the approach minimalism: that is, it works with the lay of the land as it is, with little or no major earthworks. It assumes a time before bulldozers. Doak says on his website, 'Instead of reshaping a severe slope, we try to figure out how to use it to make a golf hole interesting.'

Cape Kidnappers was a sheep station until it was bought by American billionaire Julian Robertson. Now, as a golf course, it has captured a lot of attention worldwide for its stunning aerial photographs, which reveal what Doak means when he talks about minimalism.

The 6th hole has been described by one golf writer as 'an epic par 3', justifiably so because it plays over a deep ravine from one slope to another. That it measures 206 metres from the back tee to the centre of the green means it's a fairway wood, if not a driver, for many players.

Miss slightly left here and you will face the challenge of freeing yourself from one of three pot bunkers on the hillside. Or, if my experience is anything to go by, you will watch helplessly as your new ball disappears into a steep slope covered in tall grass that's too thick to fight. This may be the toughest par-3 hole you will ever play. But the coastal view is very nice.

info

The 6th
Par 3
206 metres

Cape Kidnappers
448 Clifton Road
Te Awanga
Hawke's Bay
Tel (06) 873 1018
www.capekidnappers.com

The 13th at Cape Kidnappers

CAPE KIDNAPPERS, now with fine lodging to match the extraordinary golf course, is owned by Julian and Jose Robertson whose respective families have a long history in golf. Buying 6,000 acres of rugged, gorgeous grazing land overlooking Hawke's Bay was never intended to be a private hobby, more a love of golf they wished to share.

So it was only appropriate, you might think, that on December 22, 2003, before the golf course had opened to the public, their son Alex scored the first hole-in-one here, at the par-3 thirteenth hole. Accordingly, his name tops the Hole-in-One board inside the clubhouse. Since then the 13th has had more holes-in-one than any other par-3 hole on the course. One day there were two scored.

Australasian gannets (*Morus serrator*) at Cape Kidnappers

It is not a long hole, only 119 metres from the back tee, but it plays out along the edge of the cliff and uphill to a green that appears to drop off at the back. Moreover, it has five bunkers, and tall fescue at the back. So even though it's not long, scoring an ace here is still something to shout about.

info

The 13th
Par 3
119 metres

Cape Kidnappers
448 Clifton Road
Te Awanga
Hawke's Bay
Tel (06) 873 1018
www.capekidnappers.com

On November 1, 2007, John McCann, a visiting American golfer, scored an ace on this hole, one noted as much for the fact that his wife Mary Ellen scored a hole-in-one that day too – only hers was at the eighth, a hole that is longer and some would say more difficult.

The 14th at Cape Kidnappers

EDWARD HAWKE was one of the toughest and hardest commanders in the history of the British Navy. That he fought and defeated the French more than once was enough for him to be awarded a baronetcy. Before this, however, when Captain James Cook set sail for the South Pacific in 1768, Hawke was First Lord of the Admiralty, his boss.

In October 1769 Cook anchored off the east coast of New Zealand in a big sweeping bay. As if the place did not have a name already, he named it Hawke's Bay. He might have learned the name of the bay, Heretaunga, from Maori, had they not been preoccupied with kidnapping a Tahitian boy off Cook's ship, the *Endeavour*.

Who knows for sure what the Maori intended to do with the poor lad. In any case, shots were fired and that allowed the boy to break free and swim back to the ship.

The good Captain Cook, still in a mood for declaring place names, called the extraordinary cape that is the southern tip of Hawke's Bay Cape Kidnappers.

In 2007 the golf course here was listed by America's respected *Golf Digest* as the tenth best golf course in the world outside of the United States. The 318-metre par-4 fourteenth has a reasonably wide fairway that's easy enough to reach from the elevated tee. The trick is reaching the small, extremely rolling green with a second shot. That means making a pinpoint shot that clears the deep pot bunker in front of the green

without going too far and rolling off the back – or coming up short and, if not in the bunker, rolling off the front.

The hole has the unfortunate name 'Pimple', which may recall for some their adolescent years anguishing in front of a mirror. But the fact remains that this is one of the most difficult short par-4 holes in the country – difficult enough to make you break out all over again.

info

The 14th
Par 4
318 metres

Cape Kidnappers
448 Clifton Road
Te Awanga
Hawke's Bay
Tel (06) 873 1018
www.capekidnappers.com

The 17th at Hastings

PERHAPS BECAUSE HE DOMINATED New Zealand amateur golf for so many years, Stuart Jones was nicknamed The Emperor by the great sportswriter Terry McLean. Jones, arguably New Zealand's finest amateur of all time, took up golf only after an accidental scalding by a Wairakei geyser had shortened a developing rugby career.

A talented athlete, it didn't take Jones long to get the knack. He was on a 24 handicap when he joined the Hastings Golf Club in 1947; the following year he won the club championship.

Jones went on to win the club title more times than any club member before or since, and to represent New Zealand at the first Eisenhower Trophy, the world amateur men's team championship.

In the 1960s, Hastings, one of the best of the country's traditional club courses, hosted a series of professional tournaments sponsored by local food processing company Wattie's, and in 1965 Jones won that too.

Family business kept him from turning professional, but he remained an active player, and one Saturday, during a regular club competition, he scored a hole-in-one at the 140-metre, par-3 sixteenth hole. Next up, at the 478-metre par-5 seventeenth, he hit a solid tee shot straight down the middle of the two-tiered fairway, and followed that up with a cool second shot to about 55 metres from the pin.

It was a sensible lay-up because the green is fronted by two bunkers and flanked by two more, so reaching it in two is only for players who get a perverse joy out of sacrificing themselves on the altar of high-risk shots.

info

The 17th
Par 5
478 metres

Hastings Golf Club
1523 Maraekakaho Road
Hastings
Tel (06) 879 7206
www.hastingsgolfclub.co.nz

Stuart Jones was too smart and conservative by nature to try something like that so he laid up short of the green, took a pitching wedge out of his bag and promptly and confidently popped the ball on to the green, where it bounced once or twice before rolling into the cup for an eagle 3.

'Two eagles in a row!' he told me. 'I had never done that before and have never done it since.'

The 16th hole at Hastings

The 6th at Wairakei

WAIRAKEI INTERNATIONAL is the site of the annual Media Golf Society tournament. Once a year a motley collection of media types from around the country gather for a weekend of golf, and whatever.

Magazines have been known to enter teams, but when the society began more than thirty years ago it was newspaper men – and they were all men – who founded it. Because many were sports reporters, the tournament was timed to fall between the rugby and cricket seasons.

The event has evolved to include wives and other women (not to suggest any impropriety). After a practice round on the Saturday, two rounds of serious competition in Stableford format begin on Sunday, with individual and team prizes to be won. There are drinks and a meal at the end of each day.

Come Monday, after two days of golf and late nights drinking and telling tales, it's often the 6th hole at Wairakei that becomes the proverbial 'wall', when the weekend finally catches up. Speaking for myself, one begins to wish the tournament on Monday morning was nine holes, instead of eighteen.

The steep climb from the 5th green to the 6th tee can be a killer, especially if you are ten strokes over par by then. I've seen overweight, out of shape sports journalists reach the 6th tee completely out of breath – and they were using a cart.

Yet if there is a single great golf hole on this fabulous course, a personal favourite even if I take a beating here every time, the 6th is it. A par 4 about 400 metres long, it plays from an extremely elevated tee, the highest point on the course, down to a split-level fairway and then a narrow green that is surrounded on three sides by sand traps.

Big hitters commonly reach the bottom fairway, leaving them with a mid-iron into the green. The rest of us play a fairway wood from the top fairway, hoping to keep the ball in play, reach the green in three, 2-putt for a bogey, and move on. For most of us, a bogey at the 6th at Wairakei is an acceptable score, especially on a Monday.

info

The 6th
Par 4
401 metres

Wairakei International
State Highway One
Taupo
Tel (07) 374 8152
www.wairakeigolfcourse.co.nz

The 14th at Wairakei

AS ANYONE FAMILIAR WITH TAUPO will know, geothermal vents are scattered about seemingly everywhere, even on golf courses. Drill a hole thirty metres down on any fairway at Wairakei International and the likely result will be a geyser of some sort.

When golf was first played here in the early 1970s, there was a lively geyser behind the 14th green. To geothermal experts who monitored its activity, it was known as the Rogue Bore and when the golf course opened it was still active. Accordingly, the 14th hole became known as 'The Rogue'.

It's a golf hole worthy of shot-by-shot description because among all holes in New Zealand golf today it is an icon, even at a time when everything, it seems, has suddenly become 'iconic'.

The fourteenth at Wairakei is a par-5 dog-leg right over a corner bunker to a fairway with a giant pine looming, like one of those ancient tree-people, the Ents, in *The Lord Of The Rings*.

The tree rises up in the middle of the fairway, right where any normal second shot would go. It forces you to play to the right or left, although most hacks simply line up their second shot, let fly, and hope for the best, namely that the ball misses the tree, leaving them with a clear third shot to the high green. If not, *c'est la vie*. I've seen players hit the tree once and their ball ricochet back, only to watch them hit the tree again with their next shot.

Beyond the tree is an extremely elevated green, high enough to require a longer club than the distance would normally require. To reach the green in three, the shot has to be high enough and long enough to clear three deep bunkers directly in front of it. Just when you think you've struck a shot solid enough and straight enough to do that, you watch the ball land short and roll back down into one of the deep bunkers.

If the monster tree and the sand traps do not stop you, the deceptive, kidney-shaped, split-level green will, for a 3-putt here is common.

Wairakei International, designed by John Harris, Michael Wolveridge and Peter Thomson, was originally owned by the New Zealand government's Tourist Hotel Corporation. It is now privately owned, but it remains a true classic that is even better to play today than it was then. For the average player it's not an easy course on which to score well, yet no matter how high your score on the day it's always a great day out, more so if you've somehow managed to tame 'The Rogue'.

info

The 14th
Par 5
548 metres

Wairakei International
State Highway One
Taupo
Tel (07) 374 8152
www.wairakeigolf course.co.nz

The 18th at Centennial

IF YOU SUFFER FROM LOW SELF-ESTEEM it is probably best you do not play the Centennial Course at the Taupo Golf Club as that will mean having to play the 18th hole, a 210-metre par 3 from the back tee that may leave you feeling even worse about yourself – such is the reflective nature of golf.

Taupo is one of only two clubs in New Zealand with two 18-hole courses, the other being Harewood Golf Course in Christchurch. The other course at Taupo is called Tauhara, after the extinct (one hopes)

volcano that is a local landmark. You can walk up a track to the summit of this thousand-metre peak if you're feeling like a warm-up. The view is outstanding.

Tauhara, the golf course, is not only older than the Centennial Course by nearly fifty years, it is also more surreal for the steam vents that garnish the front nine.

info

The 18th
Par 3
210 metres

Taupo Golf Club
32 Centennial Drive
Taupo
Tel (07) 378 6933
www.taupogolf.co.nz

The Centennial, meanwhile, has the distinction of being the longest women's course in New Zealand – 5,524 metres. It opened in 1973, and while that makes it relatively young as far as golf courses go, it was never the kind of landscape meant for big earthworks – even if the club could have afforded them. So it plays naturally, you could say: mounds have remained mounds and gullies have remained gullies.

The 18th hole – one of the best closing holes in New Zealand golf – has both. This hole is not only among the longest par 3s in the country, it calls for a shot that is uphill and 'all carry' – an expression usually reserved for carry over water, but here it refers to a deep gully. When a tee shot falls short here, if the ball doesn't wind up in the sole bunker it will commonly roll back down the slope into the gully – and sometimes playing from down there is enough to make you feel really, really bad about yourself.

If there's an upside to the story it is that the green, if you reach it, is one of the biggest and flattest on the course. Given that the Centennial Course has played host to a number of top amateur tournaments, it's a fair guess that more than one match was all square until the players arrived here.

The 3rd at Kinloch

THE ROAD DOWN to the village of Kinloch on Lake Taupo was dusty and dirty and gravel all the way until Keith Holyoake, the prime minister of the day, bought a bach there. Then – surprise, surprise – money was found in the public coffers to have the road paved.

Kinloch might have remained a piece of political trivia had a couple of wide-eyed property developers not bought a chunk of land there and, as a way of inducing people to buy sections, decided to build a golf course.

They hired Jack Nicklaus to design the course: the same Jack Nicklaus who won seventy-three PGA tournaments and a record eighteen Majors; the same Jack Nicklaus who, apart from being the greatest golfer the world has ever known, has designed many of the finest new courses in the world.

The developers went one step further by paying the Golden Bear an extra million and change to be hands-on, including showing up at the grand opening. That is what is meant by a Jack Nicklaus Signature Golf Course. So Nicklaus turned up for the opening and a press conference, an odd affair where VIP guests outnumbered the press by about fifty to one. Then he played the front nine (the back nine was not ready) with his son, and using a portable PA system he described each hole to a large gallery following behind.

Nicklaus was sixty-six at the time and had had a hip replacement. He was not walking well. In fact, he appeared to be in some discomfort as he made his way around the nine holes. Yet incredibly, he still stroked the ball better than anyone there might have, with the exception of his son.

info

The 3rd
Par 3
169 metres

Kinloch Golf Course
713 Whangamata Road
Kinloch
Taupo
Tel (07) 377 8484
www.kinloch-golf.com

Nicklaus has not seen every golf course in New Zealand, of course, but he was right when he said Kinloch was unlike any course ever built in this country. However, when he said he designed the course 'for the average golfer', one veteran from a nearby club turned to me and said under his breath, 'What would he know about the average golfer?'

Kinloch prohibits high handicappers from playing the back tees. In fact, it might be a good idea to prohibit high handicappers from playing the course at all, such is the degree of difficulty here. Nicklaus was still swinging the club better than players half his age, but at the 169-metre par-3 third hole, a scenic spot that plays from an elevated tee over a water hazard, the greatest player who ever lived put his first shot in the drink. His second shot cleared the water, but he had taken three putts on this very fast rolling surface before his caddy picked up the ball and they moved on.

This experience has not dimmed Nicklaus's enthusiasm. In May 2008 *The New Zealand Herald* reported that he had visited five times and declared it his best course. With over two hundred other Nicklaus courses around the world, that's quite an accolade.

The 18th at Kinloch

AT THE TIME OF MY VISIT there in 2008, Kinloch – the residential sections, villa sites and golf course – were for sale following a long and arduous stop-start project that began with high hopes in 2002.

The golf course, the only Jack Nicklaus design in New Zealand, opened years late, and by 2008 whatever momentum the developers had hoped to create to sell the surrounding sites was lost. At an asking price of $57.7 million the whole business could be yours. You could play golf free for the rest of your life.

Yet for all of its financial woes, the golf course is there. It's not going anywhere any time soon, and it's hard to imagine it being left to grow over. Indeed, the month after I visited it was sold to an undisclosed purchaser for an undisclosed sum.

Kinloch is not an easy course to play. I'd go so far as to say that if your handicap is higher than 20 you may want to try the original nine-hole track down the road. Either that or come with your bag stocked with balls. Any 18-handicapper who can play a round here without losing a ball can have a copy of this book on me.

The par-5 eighteenth hole is however, I declare, the best 18th hole in New Zealand golf. It demands good shots but it doesn't seem as unfair or scary as some other holes on this course.

It is 514 metres long from the back tee, 382 metres from the front, but it's not the tee shot that figures in the mix here so much as the

second and third shots, thanks to a fairway that plays left, then right, then back left again to a peninsula green tucked into a small scenic lake.

Tom Long, the amicable pro here, told me Nicklaus had recently returned to play the full 18 holes; he had done so quietly and without fanfare, being back in the country to do some fishing in the South Island. How did he play the 18th? A drive straight down the middle of the fairway, he lays up with an 8-iron, then he puts a shot with a wedge to within a metre of the pin, finally one-putting for a birdie. Or at least that's how I imagine it.

info

The 18th
Par 5
514 metres

Kinloch Golf Course
713 Whangamata Road
Kinloch
Taupo
Tel (07) 377 8484
www.kinloch-golf.com

The 4th at Tarrangower

TAUMARUNUI PROMOTES ITSELF as The Middle of Everywhere, and in one sense that may be true, as the town is close to the geographic centre of the North Island. When this book was being written, though, the thing most people there were concerned about being in the middle of was the worst drought to strike the King Country in more than forty years.

Tarrangower, as the golf course is known (for the district in which it is located), had a serious problem for years with bore water containing too much iron. The iron was messing up the irrigation system, and leaving a hard pan beneath the surface of the green that was killing off the grass.

Not long ago the club put its collective head down and transformed a natural catchment area on the course into a pond, using a special liner that holds water and allows the club to retrieve balls. It comes into play at the 9th hole near the clubhouse. The first dive for balls took place a couple months after the new pond was in place and, as a measure of how well the average golfer plays, more than 500 balls were recovered.

However, if you are a player who seems to find water hazards no matter where they lie, do it at the 4th hole, even if the pond here rests directly in front of the green. This is a pretty par 3 with a water hazard shallow enough to walk into and retrieve your ball: you won't have to wait for the club to call in a diver.

Besides, many people will tell you the 4th, called 'The Drop' because the tee sits on a hill above the green, is the club's signature hole not only for the pond, but for the trees on the left and the small circular bunker on the right.

info

The 4th
Par 3
100 metres

Taumarunui Golf Club
Golf Road
Taumarunui
Tel (07) 896 7257
taumarunui@golf.co.nz

The hole is just over 100 metres long, but in that way it expresses a fundamental principle about scoring well in golf: it's not how *far* you hit the ball but *where* you hit it that matters most. Coming up short on this hole can mean taking off the shoes and socks and rolling up the pant legs.

The 17th at Ngamotu

IN 1980 THE NEW ZEALAND OPEN was played at the New Plymouth Golf Club's Ngamotu Links. Four of the noteworthy players included Wanganui son Simon Owen; Bay of Plenty legend Dennis 'Yogi' Clark; Irishman Eamonn Darcy, who just the week before had won the Air New Zealand Shell Open at Titirangi; and American Buddy Allin.

Allin was arguably the star attraction: he had won five times on the United States PGA Tour, and in the mid 1970s had had a top ten fin-

ish in both the US Open and the PGA Championship. Allin had played his collegiate golf at Brigham Young University with the great Johnny Miller, but more than that he had a special story to tell because he revived his professional golf career after serving as an artillery commander in the war in Vietnam.

The Open that year was the last one ever played at Ngamotu, and it marked the end of an era, in that the tournament ceased being played on club courses around the country, as had been the long tradition in New Zealand golf. Thereafter most club courses were deemed too short, the dictates of commercialism meant staging the tournament close to one of the four major cities, and the popularity of select courses such as the links at Paraparaumu Beach meant the New Zealand Amateur Championship was about as high profile a tournament as provincial clubs such as Ngamotu would ever see.

info

The 17th
Par 4
391 metres

New Plymouth Golf Club
735 Devon Road
New Plymouth
Tel (06) 755 0424
www.golfer.co.nz

At different stages of the 1980 New Zealand Open, Owen, Clark and Darcy led the field. Then on the final day, Allin, playing with Darcy, made a dramatic climb up the leader board when he knocked down five birdies in six holes on the front nine. It set up a dramatic finish between him and his Irish playing partner.

The club's centennial book reports: 'With the Irishman and the American both 13 under par for the tournament and with just three holes to play, the atmosphere was electric. Thousands of spectators lined the fairways to watch what would happen.

'Darcy cracked on the very next hole when he bunkered his approach and could not get up and down for par. The two reached the green of the long 17th hole in regulation and Allin secured the championship when he rolled in a long curling putt for birdie.'

The 17th at Ngamotu today is, from the white tee, a 391-metre par 4. Even professionals have to give the ball a couple of good cracks to get there. It's like a number of holes here – pastoral, tree-lined fairways more or less straight, no tricks or gimmicks or pot bunkers – just the longest par 4 on the course.

Buddy Allin was considered one of the best putters in the game at the time, and here he showed why when he sank that extraordinary putt at the 17th to win the last of the club-based New Zealand Opens. Allin later played on the senior tour with some success, but cancer finally forced him to quit playing. He was living in California when he died in March 2007.

The 15th at Westown

GOLF MAY HAVE BEEN invented in Scotland, but much of the slang is American. 'Birdie' (one under) is derived from nineteenth-century slang where 'bird' meant 'good'. A good shot was 'a bird of a shot'. Toasting it with a whiskey was celebrating 'a good birdie'. 'Eagle' (two under) was grander than a birdie, but an 'albatross' (three under) was better still.

Albatross didn't find its way into the lexicon of golf until after Gene Sarazen scored a two on a par 5 and won the Masters in 1935, a shot that is considered the most famous albatross in the history of golf. He described it as a 'dodo'. How did dodo become albatross? Who knows, but Peter Broadhead will forever remember his at this scenic course at the foot of Mount Taranaki.

The 15th hole is a 456-metre par 5 called 'The Wrecker'. It's not especially long but it wrecks scores, because branches from trees on the left extend over the fairway, and the irregular fairway produces uneven lies.

On August 25, 2007 Peter Broadhead, playing off a blistering 23 handicap, drove the ball down into rough in a gully. He could not see the green from where he stood over his second shot, but he knew straight away that he had made good contact. He watched the ball sail nicely over the rise and, seemingly, straight towards the green.

Two of his foursome were looking for a lost ball in the trees, but the fourth watched as Broadhead's shot rolled up and on to the green and straight into the hole. It was a most exceptional albatross on a day when

Broadhead also scored a birdie and lowered his handicap by two shots.

Birdies were in the news when 21-year-old Sarah Nicholson made history by leading the field of men and women in the 2006 Wairakei Open. Her one-shot lead came about when she made four birdies in five holes to score a 36-hole total of 138, six under par.

info

The 15th
Par 5
456 metres

Westown Golf Club
Upper Mangorei Road
New Plymouth
Tel (06) 758 6933
www.nzgolfcourses.co.nz/westown

The 10th at Manaia

BY JUNE 1867 EUROPEAN SETTLEMENT was well established in Auckland and Wellington but not so much in Taranaki. The plains east of the Waingongoro, one of the many splendid rivers flowing from Mount Taranaki to the sea, still belonged exclusively to Maori.

Given the rampant and vile destruction of Maori villages, marae and pa in Taranaki by British Constabulary in the previous couple of years, it should not have come as a surprise to anyone that two rather thick-headed surveyors who turned up one morning unannounced near Te Ngutu o Te Manu, the stronghold of Nga Ruahine chief Titokowaru, would be shot at. Both they and the military aide travelling with them were killed.

The Maori retreated to the stronghold of Titokowaru, whom historians now consider to have been second only to the legendary chief Te Kooti for his skill in guerrilla warfare.

Escalation was inevitable, if only because Titokowaru was hankering for a fight, while the British forces who came to arrest the men he was protecting were led by Major Gustavus von Tempsky, a mad-dog Prussian more than willing to throw himself into a fray, any fray.

The south Taranaki war, one of the final phases of the Taranaki Wars, lasted about a year but its legacies are scattered about the province today. Many of them are earthly fortifications, but the one at the 10th hole of the Manaia Golf Club is different.

This hole is one of the shortest par 4s in the country. It is only 230 metres long, and were it not for the pine trees even I might be capable of reaching the green in one. But it is a dog-leg around the trees – trees that are too tall for most of us to hit over – so for most all that's required is a fairway wood from the tee and a short iron to reach the green.

On the other hand, if you slice your tee shot you may strike a blow in memory of Titokowaru, for over there is a British redoubt and the recreation of a British watchtower. It's easy to imagine that it was from here that the constabulary, led by the irrepressible, sword-waving von Tempsky, departed for Te Ngutu o Te Manu, where they would suffer an embarrassing defeat. Von Tempsky was shot in the head and died a painful death in the bush on a cold and wet September morning in 1868. His body was burned on a funeral pyre.

info

The 10th
Par 4
230 metres

Manaia Golf Club
Bennett Drive
Manaia
Tel (06) 274 8325
manaia@golf.co.nz

The 3rd at Belmont Links

THAT BLOODY HILL. It sits out there off the 3rd tee blocking a view of the town. And worse, it makes scoring par on this 375-metre par 4 even more difficult. It's no wonder some of the club's members voted to have the damn thing removed.

Belmont Links, as the Wanganui Golf Club is known, is one of a handful of clubs formed in the 1890s. It has played host to nine New Zealand Opens and seven New Zealand Amateur Championships and is considered one of the finest golf courses in the land. The club recently re-numbered the holes, but when they made the original 6th the 3rd they decided to remove the hill. It was still there as this book was going to print, but the greenkeeper, Barry Shannon, led me to believe it would be gone soon, and not too soon for some.

Removal of the hill will mean a direct line of sight from tee to green, which should ease the mind some. But more than that it will give this historic golf course its most scenic hole, for in the line of vision from the tee and beyond the green will be Wanganui, the River City.

Wanganui is where Peter Snell broke the world record for the mile, running 3.54.4 minutes at Cooks Gardens on a grass track on January 27, 1962. Indeed, the track at Cooks Gardens is as historic as the golf course, although to the best of my knowledge no world records have been broken at Belmont Links.

In 1911, the first Open played here was won by Arthur Duncan, one

of New Zealand's greatest amateur players of the early 20th century. In 1929, the Open was won by Andrew Shaw, the first of six victories for the man who would dominate New Zealand golf in the 1930s. The last Open played here was won by Australian Bob Shearer in 1978.

Who knows? Maybe there's a world record of some kind in all of that, ready to be uncovered by a dedicated golf historian. For now it's noted that once that hill is gone, the tee at Wanganui's new 3rd will have a very pleasant outlook.

info

The 3rd
Par 4
375 metres

Wanganui Golf Club
Clarkson Avenue
Wanganui
Tel (06) 349 0559
www.wanganuigolfclub.co.nz

The 18th at Rangatira

AS THE RANGITIKEI RIVER makes its way down from the Central Plateau to the Tasman Sea, it splits the bottom half of the North Island in two. Along the way it leaves some of the most dramatic gorges, canyons and cliffs imaginable.

A few kilometres south of Taihape a company called Mokai Gravity Canyon claims to have the most extreme flying fox in the world. Check out the flying fox at Gravity Canyon if you must, but keep in mind that

the Rangatira Golf Club, just a little further south on State Highway One, is the only golf course in the country that has its own such conveyance – albeit of a somewhat less hair-raising type.

Rangitira plays on three different levels, as it was built on terraces, scoured out over the years by the river. The first six holes play on the top level, the next six on the second tier, and the final six at the bottom. It's from the bottom, after putting out on the 18th hole, that players get back to the top using Bernie's Bomb.

The 18th is a short par 4, only 320 metres long from the tips, so the trick is to hit the ball as straight as possible to avoid getting stuck under any of the native trees that shape the fairway. It's also a slight dog-leg to a sloping green and there's no sand to hold you up. In fact, Rangatira has no bunkers at all, which might usually suggest a rather boring little track, but here, because of the river scene and Bernie's Bomb, that's hardly the case.

Bernie's Bomb is, in reality, an electric cable car that carries players back up an incline rail to the top. It can hold up to four people and their buggies, and is named for the man who built it in the 1970s – although it's been reconditioned many times since then.

info

The 18th
Par 4
320 metres

Rangatira Golf Club
State Highway One
Hunterville
Tel (06) 322 9859
www.rangatiragolf.co.nz

The 7th at Rangitikei

ONE OF THE GREATEST FINISHES for victory in the history of golf was by Palmerston North-born Craig Perks. It happened at the 2002 Players Championship, and because the Players is regarded by many as a fifth major, along with The Masters, the US Open, the Open Championship and the PGA, this made Perks' extraordinary play at the final three holes that much more special.

Perks played a lot of golf in the Manawatu before accepting a golf scholarship to the University of Southwestern Louisiana (now the University of Louisiana at Lafayette). After a successful collegiate career, he turned professional in 1993. For six years he toiled on minor tours before qualifying for the PGA Tour in 1999.

The 2002 Players was played, as it has been for many years now, at the TPC Sawgrass at Ponte Vedra Beach, Florida, a course designed by Pete Dye, one of the world's finest golf architects. Dye set a new standard in course design when he unveiled the island-green at the 17th hole there. It is now one of the most famous golf holes in the world.

In 2002, Craig Perks came to the 16th hole at TPC Sawgrass one shot behind the leaders. Suddenly, American television commentators were talking about New Zealand in a way they had not done since Bob Charles, but they didn't have long to elaborate because, in a flash, Perks chipped in for an eagle and instantly became the tournament leader.

The next hole, the 17th, was a par 3 with a green set out on an

island and only a thin walkway for players and caddies to access it. With hundreds of thousands of dollars on the line, many players have come to that point in the Players only to watch their tee shot fall short into the lake, or bounce into the lake off the back of the green. Craig Perks, though, managed to land his ball on the green, then roll in an improbable nine-metre putt for a birdie.

info

The 7th
Par 4
335 metres

Rangitikei Golf Club
Raumai Road
Bulls
Tel (06) 322 1475
www.rangitikei.nzgolf.net

As if to show no fear, at the 18th and final hole Perks *chipped* in from about nine metres behind the green to secure his famous win. He won US$1.1 million and became one of golf's better known television highlight reels. Unfortunately, that win turned out to be his only victory on the tour, and in 2007 he announced his retirement.

At the Rangitikei Golf Club, a quiet links near Bulls, a photo of Perks winning the Players adorns the clubhouse wall, along with a note from him describing Rangitikei as 'my favourite golf course anywhere in the world'.

Another golfer fond of Rangitikei is Tim Wilkinson. In 2008 Wilkinson made the PGA Tour, and at the Sony Open in Hawai'i shot to fame with an incredible third-round 62: eight birdies and ten pars. But it was at Rangitikei that, at fifteen, he first broke par, shooting three under.

The 7th hole at Rangitikei is a short par 4, but it plays straight up a hill to a blind green. Although it is the No. 2 stroke hole on the course, for many the hill makes it No. 1. Perhaps it is because of the blind green, or just the hill itself, but no one has ever scored an eagle here, not even Craig Perks.

The 13th at Hokowhitu

THE MANAWATU GOLF CLUB, home of some of the most successful New Zealand professionals, namely Grant Waite, Craig Perks and Tim Wilkinson, has also had a number of celebrity guests over the years. American country singer Glenn Campbell, British comedian Ronnie Corbett and England cricketer Geoff Boycott have all played at this Palmerston North course.

Part of the reason for the club's success is that, as well as being one of the most attractive golf courses in the country, it is also one of the oldest. It has played host to five New Zealand Opens and eight New Zealand Amateur championships.

Popularly known as Hokowhitu, the club celebrated its centenary in 1995 with a book that recalled the 1973 occasion when Bob Charles won the last of his four New Zealand Open titles here. After an opening round 72, an unhappy Charles, trailing Australians Peter Thomson, Kel Nagle and Ian Stanley, grumbled to some club members about the conditions of the greens. The great sports writer Terry McLean, reporting for *New Zealand Golf News*, shrewdly observed that after the first round 'Charlie' went on to score his rounds in 30, 28, 31 and 30 putts, and 'that superlatively consistent putting would simply not have been possible had the greens been as bad as he contended.'

McLean called it right, as he usually did, because by Sunday Charles had overtaken Thomson and Nagle, and by the time he teed off on the

back nine he had only Ian Stanley to contend with. Stanley, a flamboyant character in a sport that can be restrained, let his temper get the best of him after three-putting one hole then dropping shots at the next two.

The 13th at Manawatu is not among the longest par-4 holes on the course, but it has a kink in it, and an irregular fairway shaped by the movement of the Waikato River. A large sand trap guards the green on the left. It was here that Charles effectively closed the deal on the 1973 New Zealand Open when he sank a long birdie putt that gave him a four-shot lead over Stanley, who never regained his composure.

If Bob Charles' reputation as the greatest Kiwi golfer was not in place by then, it certainly was after he was seen winning that tournament – it was the first golf tournament in New Zealand to be broadcast live and in colour on national television.

info

The 13th
Par 4
325 metres

Manawatu Golf Club
Centennial Drive
Palmerston North
Tel (06) 357 8793
www.manawatugolfclub.co.nz

The 15th at Levin

IT'S GOING ON TWENTY YEARS NOW since Nick Cooper started the garden. Cooper is a chartered accountant in Levin, and a regular for Thursday night golf at the Levin Golf Club.

When the club bulldozed a bank at the back of the course to make way for a second tee at the 15th hole – a higher tee, and one, as it turned out, with an outlook enhanced by Lake Horowhenua – Cooper thought the bare ground looked so unseemly he had to do something about it. He planted agapanthus and canna lilies. Today the garden has grown to such a size it could pass for an official botanic garden, and it is one of the features visitors remember about the course after playing a round of golf here.

This nearly ended one cool August night not too long ago. For two decades Cooper had volunteered his time to keep up the garden, and on this night, after one of his regular Thursday rounds, he was weeding after dark when black clouds produced a bolt of lightning so close it shook the ground he was standing on.

The 15th hole by the garden is a par 4, only 320 metres long from the white tee. It plays straight, and finishes at a pancake green with no bunkers. As if to make the hole friendlier, the club has removed a row of pines down the left.

Levin is a relaxing links in peaceful countryside not far from the sea, but imagine walking after dark down the 15th fairway, in the far

corner of the golf course, with a black sky hovering above and lightning crackling.

The last thing on Nick Cooper's mind as he walked back to his car that night was not his fine garden, or even how he might go about scoring at least par the next time he played the hole. It was how lucky he was not to have been killed.

info

The 15th
Par 4
320 metres

Levin Golf Club
Moutere Road
Levin
Tel (06) 368 6189
www.levinlinksgolf.co.nz

The 18th at Paraparaumu Beach

GRANT WAITE WAS BORN IN AUSTRALIA, but he moved to New Zealand at a young age and before long was playing golf at the Manawatu Golf Club. By the time he left school, he was good enough to attract the attention of the University of Oklahoma, where he played on a golf scholarship until he turned professional in 1987.

It took a few years, but Waite's PGA Tour career finally took off in 1993 when he won the Kemper Open in Potomac, Maryland. Three years later he fell short of winning the Phoenix Open, but he did shoot an incredible 60 on the last day – the second best Sunday round in PGA Tour history. (The best remains David Duval's 59.)

Waite, now a United States citizen, has struggled to stay on top of his game since those peak years in the 1990s, but against all odds he has made more than US$4 million in career earnings. And it was against all odds that he will always be remembered in New Zealand for his shot on the 18th at Paraparaumu Beach on the Friday of the 1992 New Zealand Open.

Paraparaumu Beach Golf Club is simply one of the finest links courses in the world. It may not be as old as the links courses of Scotland, or have their legendary status, but it has the qualities of the best links courses. That's why it has been listed as the favourite New Zealand golf course among touring professionals, including US Open winner Michael Campbell.

The course was designed by Australian Alex Russell, who worked for many years with the legendary English golf course designer Alister MacKenzie. It has hosted twelve New Zealand Opens, five of them won by New Zealanders: Bob Charles, Greg Turner, Michael Long, Michael Campbell and Grant Waite.

The 18th hole at Paraparaumu Beach could be a friendlier par 5 if the club took out all the bunkers and the lateral water hazard down the right, but I suspect they won't do that because the hole is not especially long, just over 500 metres from the tips.

Grant Waite was considered by some to have a weak short game but a long and accurate game off the tee: that is, he could drive the ball with the best of them but he couldn't putt consistently well. Sometimes, however, his long game was so good he didn't have to putt at all.

On the 18th on the Friday of the 1992 New Zealand Open, Waite drove his ball clear of any hazard to a position that left him a clear shot at the green. Using a two-iron, he struck the ball cleanly and left everyone in the gallery that day with the story of a lifetime, for as they watched his ball rolled on to the green, up a gentle slope, and into the hole.

Waite carried on to win the tournament. Today, when you play this hole (as you must) keep an eye out for the plaque in the ground from where he hit the shot. It remains the club's first and only albatross scored on that hole.

info

The 18th
Par 5
500 metres

Paraparaumu Beach Golf Club
376 Kapiti Road
Paraparaumu Beach
Tel (04) 902 8216
www.paraparaumubeachgolfclub.co.nz

The 15th at Titahi

TITAHI (FORMERLY TITAHI BAY) is a nine-hole course with eighteen tees: eighteen tees playing to nine greens. The course is famous, for this is where 2005 United States Open winner Michael Campbell began playing golf: his father Tom was a member. Less well-known is that members of the Springboks rugby team played at the original course during their 1937 tour, and that during the Second World War the site was used as a camp for American Marines preparing for and recovering from action in the Pacific. The course on its new site opened in 1958.

Titahi is less famous for being the first golf course I played in New Zealand after arriving from the United States for the first time in December 1971. It was then as much sheep paddock as golf course; the greens had an electric fence around them, as I learned the hard way. But the coastal view from that promontory was worth the visit, with or without golf clubs.

Today the sheep are gone and the course, resurfaced, looks every bit as though it is being looked after by a pro. I am also willing to bet it is the only golf course in the world that can claim scores on a par 4 at the same time from a foursome of four, three, two and a hole-in-one.

In the late 1990s, the foursome of Steven Askew, Rob Percival, Steven Kershaw and Darryl Pulman were playing in a club competition on a day with a slight bit of wind at their backs when they stepped up to the tee at the par-4 fifteenth hole. The hole is about 240 metres long and drive-

Callaway
GOLF
cambo

able for big hitters. The only problem is there's no roll, because the green is elevated with a steep bank of rough in front. There are also out of bounds and a grove of trees tight on the left. The slightest pull means the ball may never be seen again.

This is one of those irregular golf holes that challenge the mind as much as the swing, and this makes the feat of that foursome even more remarkable.

info

The 15th
Par 4
240 metres

Titahi Golf Club
Gloaming Hill
Titahi Bay
Tel (04) 236 7334
www.titahigolf.com

The law of probability says that on any given hole and among any given foursome there will be at least one weak-kneed hack who will lose it completely when faced with an irregularity. Not so in this instance. Darryl Pulman missed the green in front, but chipped through the back of the green, chipped back to within about six feet and sunk his putt for four. Steven Kershaw drove the green and two-putted for a birdie. Rob Percival drove the green and one-putted for an eagle. Steven Askew drove the green and scored a hole-in-one.

The 14th at Mahunga

THE GHOST OF A MAORI MAN, believed to be from the early nineteenth century, used to appear on this course, which lies on the banks of the Waipoua River. It was laid to rest once and for all in 2000 with a ceremonial karakia, or prayer.

Who was he? Kaikokirikiri Pa, part of which was on the site where the golf course is today, was the stronghold of a Rangitane chief, Retimana Te Korou. Around 1834 the pa was invaded by marauding Te Ati Awa from Taranaki and Te Korou was taken captive. As he was being taken south along the coast he escaped near the Orongorongo River, after whacking one of his captors, Te Wera of Ngati Mutunga, with a tomahawk. It is possible that the ghost was one of his hapu who was less lucky – it is said the stream running through the course ran with blood.

After living with his family in exile on Mahia Peninsula near Wairoa, Te Korou returned to the Wairarapa in the 1840s, following the signing of a peace agreement with Taranaki tribes in the Hutt Valley. He became a Christian – he and his family were baptised by the missionary William Colenso – and later sold some of his land to the English cooper Joseph Masters, founder of the Small Farms Association. In 1854 this collective founded the town of Masterton.

Remains of Te Korou's pa – mainly indentations of storage pits, whare sites and fortification posts – can be seen between the 10th

Retimana Te Korou; portrait by Gottfried Lindauer

info

The 14th
Par 5
390 metres

Mahunga Golf Club
Oxford Street
Masterton
Tel (06) 377 4990
www.mahungagolf.com

green and the 11th tee, and if the ghost ever makes a comeback it may be here.

Or he may appear on the 14th, one of the shortest par 5s in the country. It is only 390 metres long, and straight, more or less. For big hitters reaching the green in two is no sweat, but there is a catch: the approach on this hole has to clear the ill-fated stream.

Te Korou lived a long life: when he died he was said to be over a hundred. By then he was such a respected figure in the Wairarapa that many leading settlers joined the cortège of 300 people to his burial. His grave lies in Masterton Cemetery, only a few metres from that of Joseph Masters.

In the 1970s Retimana Reserve was established on the northern outskirts of Masterton, but interestingly it sits below Lansdowne Hill, closer to the Masterton Golf Club's Lansdowne golf course than to Mahunga.

The 11th at Lansdowne

ONE WELL-KNOWN NAME associated with Lansdowne, the Masterton Golf Club, is Bob (later Sir Bob) Charles. Charles was a thin-as-a-rail teenage bank teller when he lived and played in Masterton. Although he later moved to the South Island and played out of the Christchurch Golf Club, Lansdowne can justifiably claim to be his home, for it was here he honed his game in such a way as to win the New Zealand Open against an impressive international field at Heretaunga at the age of eighteen.

But there always was, and will be, more than one name associated with the Masterton Golf Club, as there ought to be for a club that's been around since 1899. Take Charlie Liverton for example. Charlie was a club standout, not so much for his scoring ability as for his 'course management': he commonly played a round with a bottle of gin in his bag, and the more he drank the better he played.

Not so his fellow players – at least, those who found it impossible to refuse Charlie when he offered them a drink. About the time they reached the 11th hole Charlie usually had the match in the bag, while his inebriated opponents were struggling just to complete the round.

Lansdowne plays over hills above the town. The 11th is a par 3 along the outer edge, with sweeping views of Masterton and the eastern hills. The small green has a grass bank on the left and an extremely sharp drop-off on the right. Bounce the ball off the left bank and wind up

on the green; bounce it off the right bank and your playing partners may never see you again.

One club member, Noel Preston, scored the only hole-in-one in his life on this hole, but it wasn't on the day a few years ago when he turned up here in a match against Charlie Liverton. That day Charlie asked Noel if he'd like another sip of the gin. Noel said, 'Ah, why not?' And that was it: according to legend, poor ol' Noel played not another hole that day.

info

The 11th
Par 3
160 metres

Masterton Golf Club
Manuka Street
and Boltons Road
Masterton
Tel (06) 377 4984
www.mastergolf.org.nz

The 3rd at Martinborough

THE STORY OF WINEMAKING in the Wairarapa is said to have begun in 1978, when publisher and *bon vivant* Alister Taylor planted chardonnay and gewürztraminer on the river terraces of his property in Martinborough. He was aiming to make his own wine, a truly novel thing to do at that time in New Zealand.

Taylor, who in 1971 had published the book *Bullshit and Jellybeans* by radical activist Tim Shadbolt (now the sedate mayor of Invercargill), was a colourful character so the story's stuck, but in fact the first person to plant grapes in the Wairarapa was Englishman William Beetham. Beetham began planting pinot meunier and hermitage grapes on his land near Masterton in 1883. Had it not been for the prohibition movement, the wine industry he began might have thrived.

Since Taylor, with the help of government scientists, discovered that the soil and climate of Martinborough were similar to those of Burgundy, this delightful town has become one of the country's premier winemaking regions, and the only one that can be described as a wine village – such is its charm. Toast Martinborough, a wine and food festival held here every November, is one of the most popular of the many such festivals that inhabit every corner of New Zealand today.

Toast Martinborough includes a tournament at the Martinborough Golf Club, a course characterised by such a diverse range of beautiful

Martinborough golf course, from a hot air balloon

trees that it could be mistaken for an English country estate.

The stars of the show are the English oaks. These magnificent trees can be seen from the tee at the 340-metre, par-4 third hole, but they are too removed from the fairway to cause concern to anyone who can hit a golf ball reasonably straight.

info

The 3rd
Par 4
340 metres

Martinborough Golf Club
Todd's Road
Martinborough
Tel (06) 306 9076
www.martinboroughgolfclub.co.nz

However, the third, modest in every way, plays along a boundary next to the road – and across the road, if you need a reminder of what really matters in these parts, is a vineyard of Palliser Estate Wines, exposed and defenceless to a slice. As you can imagine, such a shot is not at all uncommon during the Toast Martinborough golf tournament.

The 1st at Te Marua

FROM WELLINGTON, Te Marua golf course is a few minutes north of Upper Hutt on State Highway Two, at the foot of the Rimutaka Range.

If there's a singular feature shaping this course it's the Hutt River carving its way through the hills. On the brightest of days, the river sparkles. It can be seen from a number of spots on the course, but the best view is from the first tee – a hole that, because of the river, is one of the most idiosyncratic in the country. A par 4, from its elevated tee the hole plays across the river to a fairway running away to the left. Altogether, this makes the first shot of the day something of a tricky challenge.

For a time the first at Te Marua was made even trickier by the presence of a dog, Shadow, which belonged to Bruce Hicks, the club's manager from the late 1980s to early 1990s. Shadow was a border collie, a breed that has especially good eyesight, so it wasn't hard for Shadow to follow the flight of a golf ball. The only problem was Shadow enjoyed this so much he would sit directly in front of the first tee to watch players tee off.

It was no use trying to chase the dog away: that was her spot. She wasn't about to move and everyone knew it. So the regulars who knew the score simply accepted the presence of a dog taking its life into its own hands – and if, by chance, someone drove the ball too low and Shadow tried to catch it…

It is a testament to the quality of players at Te Marua – and maybe to Shadow for knowing which ones to stay clear of – that for all the years Shadow sat in front of the first tee watching players tee off, she never got badly beaned. According to Hicks she did get thumped once, but that was by someone practising chip shots and Shadow was able to regain her senses pretty quickly.

info

The 1st
Par 4
360 metres

Te Marua Golf Club
State Highway 2
Upper Hutt
Tel (04) 526 7020
www.temaruagolfclub.co.nz

Incidentally, Shadow was not alone in her canine fondness for golf. In 2008, BBC News reported that Oscar, a black Labrador in Scotland, had had thirteen golf balls removed after his owner heard rattling noises coming from the dog's stomach. Oscar and his master regularly took a stroll near Pitreavie Golf Club in Dunfermline, Fife, a course designed by the legendary Alister MacKenzie, not that the good doctor was to blame.

But the record must go to Libby, a German shepherd whose owner worked at Didsbury Golf Club in Manchester. When Libby became ill, doctors operated and found she had swallowed no fewer than twenty-eight golf balls.

The 10th at Heretaunga

FROM HER COLOURFUL SHOES to her choice of hats, Jocelyn Hornabrook will be remembered as one of the best and most stylish women ever to play golf in New Zealand.

She grew up in Masterton and learned the game from her parents, who were members of the Masterton Golf Club, Lansdowne, before they moved to Wellington. There, playing out of the Royal Wellington Golf Club – known to one and all as Heretaunga – Jocelyn became one of the best female players in the country. In the 1930s and '40s she played for Wellington in twelve consecutive national provincial championships, and from 1955 to 1974 she won the Royal Wellington club title nine times.

The 10th hole at Heretaunga has plenty of stories to tell, for the course has been the site of seven New Zealand Opens and a number of men's and women's amateur championships. But in 1992 Jocelyn Hornabrook was seventy-eight years old and still playing regularly when she stepped up to the tee here one Sunday afternoon.

The hole is a par 3, and only 93 metres long for women, but it plays uphill to a green with a false front, meaning shots commonly fall short and roll back into the abyss. The green also has a couple of grass mounds waiting to kick any errant tee shot away.

As Jocelyn Hornabrook would later tell a reporter, she teed off with a six-iron.

'There was a man waving his arms up on the green just after I played my shot. I could not see what had happened as the green is higher than the tee.

'It was not until we got up on the green that I saw two balls [belonging to her playing partners]. When I had a look in the hole, there was my ball. It was just a fluke. You could say I was lucky.'

info

The 10th
Par 3
143 metres

Royal Wellington Golf Club
28 Golf Road
Heretaunga
Lower Hutt
Tel (04) 528 4590
www.rwgc.co.nz

Maybe, maybe not, for that was Jocelyn Hornabrook's third hole-in-one on the 10th at Heretaunga, and her fifth overall.

The 10th at Hutt

DAVE THOMAS was the most famous Welsh golfer of the 1950s and '60s. In 1958 he lost a play-off to Peter Thomson at the British Open. In 1961 he again came close to winning that major championship when he finished one shot behind Jack Nicklaus.

He won elsewhere, however, and appeared for Great Britain in the Ryder Cup four times before retiring from competitive golf to design courses. His work includes The Belfry in the West Midlands, Terre Blanche in Provence, St Leon-Rot in Baden-Württemberg, and a re-shaping of Turnberry Isle in Florida.

In the late 1950s, Thomas played in New Zealand. He had come for a tournament at Paraparaumu Beach, but while he was in Wellington he played an exhibition match at the Hutt Golf Club, a solid choice because Hutt is the oldest club in the North Island.

Established in 1892, Hutt has been at its present site since 1908. For many years the current 10th hole there was the first. Today it is a par 3, but when Dave Thomas played here it was a very short par 4.

By then the lower Hutt Valley was rapidly developing into a new suburb. At the Hutt Golf Club the first hole was being squeezed by a housing development, although directly behind the green was a brick house that had been there since before the war.

Neil Woodbury, a long-standing member of the club who saw the Dave Thomas match, described Thomas as 'built like a rugby lock and

renowned for his length from the tee' – which may leave you wondering if Thomas was showing off the day he stepped up to the first tee at Hutt and pulled a driver from his bag.

Fine, Thomas wanted to impress people: that is what exhibitions are all about, especially exhibitions by Welsh golfers, who don't get the chance often. He set up and took a mighty swing. The ball sailed over the green, ricocheted off the brick house and bounced back out on to the green, where Thomas impressed even himself by two-putting for a birdie.

Local amateurs tried to emulate Thomas's feat, a trend that in time effectively put an end to the first being a short par 4. By then too many

houses were being threatened by determined hacks. John Harris, who would later become best known for his work in building Wairakei International, was called in to make a change. He turned the par-4 first hole into the par-3 tenth that it is today, brought into play a water hazard – and, for their location in the line of flight, some of New Zealand golf's most notorious trees.

info

The 10th
Par 3
177 metres

Hutt Golf Club
Military Road
Lower Hutt
Tel (04) 567 4722
www.huttgolfclub.co.nz

The 1st at Miramar

'THAT'S A SHIT OF A HOLE,' one member told me when I casually asked about the 347-metre, par-4 opening hole at the Miramar Golf Club. I knew that of course, but here 'shit' can mean good, maybe even great, certainly memorable when the hole is played in a northerly – Wellington's prevailing wind.

In 1993 the club commissioned Australian Graham Marsh to redesign the course, and in 1995 his masterpiece was unveiled. What had been a scratchy, if historic, little track next to the airport before Marsh worked his magic is now one of the finest links courses in the land, even if it's battered by gales and the sound of jet engines.

Graham Marsh remains one of Australia's finest players. As recently as 1997 he won the US Senior Open, his seventh career win in the United States, in a career with more than sixty titles worldwide, including the World Match Play and New Zealand PGA championship.

His design portfolio today includes a host of terrific golf courses around the world, but then I'm biased towards pot bunkers. Trying to get the ball out of them is never any fun. Pot bunkers, so deep you can get lost down there, force you to give up a shot like no other sand trap in the game. But unlike conventional bunkers, they bring a touch of old-world to a course like nothing else.

The first at Miramar *is* a shit of a hole, especially in a capital wind. A stream down the right and a pot bunker at the corner of the dog-leg

wait to punish those who push the ball to the right, or think they can go left and cut the corners. There are more pot bunkers to contend with, guarding a slick two-tiered green. In a northerly, with the wind in your face, it's easy enough to imagine someone winning this hole with a triple bogey. Things, you may think, can only get better.

info

The 1st
Par 4
347 metres

Miramar Golf Club
1 Stewart Duff Drive
Miramar
Wellington
Tel (04) 801 7649
www.miramargolfclub.co.nz

The 6th at Nelson

THE TASMAN BAY is not only shaped like a V for victory, but here 'victory' can unfold in the most unusual ways. Tasman Bay, or more specifically Blind Channel, shapes the outer boundary of the Nelson Golf Club.

The club's seaside location and the fact that it sits directly in the flight path of planes landing at Nelson Airport, mean the golf course combines the best qualities of a links course with sound effects from *Battle Of Britain*. Try putting for par with a plane descending fast and loud over your head.

info

The 6th
Par 3
166 metres

Nelson Golf Club
Bolt Road
Nelson
Tel (03) 548 5028
www.nelsongolf.co.nz

On the most extraordinary of days, however, putting isn't necessary at the 6th hole, a par 3 that is 166 metres long from the tips. If anyone should ever compile a list of the best par-3 holes in the South Island, this one would be a sitter. It plays along the shoreline of the aptly named Blind Channel to the right of two pot bunkers and a kidney-shaped green.

This hole has seen what must surely rank among the most bizarre holes-in-one. The tide was out on the day club member Tom Pyatt stepped up to the 6th tee. Pyatt chose to play from the white tee, 142 metres from the pin. His tee shot sailed right, out over the shoreline and into the mudflat. All appeared lost, but miraculously the ball struck a rock and ricocheted back high in the air, finally landing on the edge of the green, from where it rolled into the cup.

The 13th at Greenacres

IF THERE WERE AN AWARD for the most deceptive golf hole in New Zealand – one that looks easy but plays like a bad storm – this hole at Greenacres, near Richmond in Nelson, would be a strong contender.

It has many hard luck stories to tell. Even members who know it well can be playing along nicely through twelve holes, then come to this – one of the shortest par 4s in the South Island, only 300 metres from the back tees – and have all hell break loose.

As they approach they feel a little nervous: they know what lies ahead. It doesn't matter that the hole is called 'Hideaway' – they know where to find it. What they don't always know is *how* to find it.

This is a short dog-leg to the left that needs a mere long iron or fairway wood off the tee. Some may use a driver, but for even the average player a driver could be too long because a solid smack will send the ball flying through the dog-leg and across the fairway into trouble.

The real fun begins with the approach shot. From the dog-leg it may be a mere short iron to the green, but this green is long and narrow and extremely elevated. And if that's not enough, it slopes away in two different directions. Missing the green means trying to chip the ball up on to it from what can be deep rough and other near impossible positions. As one club member told me: 'I've seen people chip from one side of that green to the other, the ball rolling off again each time, until they give up and move on.'

The royal spoonbill (*Platalea leucorodia regia*)

Greenacres is a placid links on the shores of the Waimea Estuary, a tidal waterway that flows gently into Tasman Bay. There was nothing placid or gentle, however, about the hotshot scratch player who turned up here one day for a tournament he expected to win. He was playing like a pro, and sure enough he was leading the field – until he reached the 13th. Fit to be tied, he was lucky to escape with a triple bogey.

info

The 13th
Par 4
300 metres

Greenacres Golf Club
Best Island
Nelson
Tel (03) 544 6441
www.greenacresgolfclub.co.nz

Waimea is one of New Zealand's largest estuaries, and a biological treasure trove. Because of its rich resources, Maori lived here from the 1500s, and thirty-three archaeological sites have been found. The mud flats make a perfect habitat for shorebirds, and the estuary is classed as of international importance for migratory birds. So if you need to erase the memory of the 13th, a spot of bird-watching could work wonders. Look out for white herons, royal spoonbills and variable oystercatchers.

The 14th at Clearwater

THE SOUTHERN ALPS rise up majestically in the distance, but just as snow-covered peaks are exhilarating against a clear blue sky, when it comes to golf, mountains can be like the ghostly spirit that rises up out of sand in *Raiders Of The Lost Ark*. In this film the Nazis open what's supposed to be the source of eternal life. At first the spirit appears to be a beautiful woman, only to turn suddenly into the face of death.

This is what it can be like playing a golf course where conditions are affected by mountains. Playing Clearwater in the morning can be a completely different experience from playing there after lunch. Just ask the host of top professionals who turn up each year for the combined New Zealand PGA Championship/Nationwide Tour event. The difference between a morning and afternoon tee time can be the difference between winning a lot of money and nothing at all.

Clearwater, a Peppers resort five minutes from Christchurch Airport, is one of the finest golf courses in New Zealand – on a fine day, a day with plenty of sunshine and no wind, no rain. I've been told they happen. The course is a credit to Queenstown's John Darby, who designed it in consultation with Bob Charles. Darby also designed Millbrook Resort, The Hills and Jack's Point – all near Queenstown.

Because the big tournament at Clearwater each year is part of the US PGA's Nationwide Tour, and one of only three on the tour played outside the United States, it is reported worldwide. Accordingly, Christchurch,

one of its main supporters, also gets a truckload of publicity, with images of this English-style garden city flashed around the world.

The 14th hole at Clearwater is one of the most quirky par 5s in the land, wind or no wind, rain or no rain.

It is actually three fairways: a meandering stream divides the land in a way reminiscent of the south of England. The hole is 475 metres long, not so long for a par 5, but to clear the first traverse of the stream takes a drive of about 180 metres on the fly – too far for the average hack, especially in the wind.

The sensible thing to do is lay up and hope for a solid second shot to the next fairway, defined by a second cut by the stream. That leaves a third shot to an elevated green set slightly off to the left.

Wind and rain can break a golf course, but no matter the conditions this example of target golf – as opposed to rip, shit and bust – is surely among the top ten par 5s in New Zealand.

info

The 14th
Par 5
475 metres

Clearwater Resort
Clearwater Avenue
Harewood
Christchurch
Tel (03) 360 2146
www.clearwaternz.com

Nicholas Thompson (US) celebrates his win at the NZ PGA Championship at Clearwater, 2007.

The 1st at Windsor

THERE'S A BIZARRE GAME, known to be played in the most out of the way places, called GolfCross. I've never seen it played so I can report only what I've been told by usually reliable sources: that GolfCross is a combination of golf and rugby.

To score points, a player must strike a 'golf ball' shaped like a miniature rugby ball through a set of goalposts, a kind of a netted goal in the air. The aim is to hit a 'field goal' – if you can imagine.

I was told by Burton Silver, the enterprising New Zealander who created the 'sport' (that's what he called it), that he hoped to export it, franchise it and retire young. Good luck to him. Silver wrote a book called *Why Cats Paint* that became an international bestseller, so maybe he knows something.

If GolfCross catches on, the first hole at the Windsor Golf Club in Christchurch, with its two giant poplars, could attract a lot of cash in the coming years. Perhaps it's the Englishness of Canterbury but there seem to be more poplar trees in the province than in any other place in New Zealand, and many of them can be found at the Windsor Golf Club – where these two frame the first hole like goalposts.

It has been said that the par-3 opening hole at Windsor is the toughest first hole in New Zealand golf. The average score here over the years is reportedly 4.35, which suggests that is true, and maybe the two poplar trees have something to do with that.

The first thing that goes on in the minds of players, even some who have played here all their lives, is: Can I get through those damn trees and have a shot at reaching the green? Am I Grant Fox, or that other fellow who made only one test appearance?

The hole plays up a slope to a two-tiered green about 160 metres away, which means the average golfer drives the ball with a long iron or fairway wood, trying not to swing so hard that you pull the ball over a fence and into out of bounds tight on the left.

This may be the toughest first hole in New Zealand because you can't beat it with just a field goal: you have to score a try too. I wasn't surprised to learn from one club member that, while players often 'kick a field goal' on this hole, no one to his knowledge has ever scored a hole-in-one.

info

The 1st
Par 3
160 metres

Windsor Golf Club
115 Waitikiri Drive
Burwood
Christchurch
Tel (03) 383 1403
www.windsorgolf.co.nz

The 4th at Shirley

UNTIL THAT MEMORABLE DAY at the Shirley Links of the Christchurch Golf Club, Mick Boon was better known for his cricket. He was a wicketkeeper for Canterbury in the 1920s, and even played for New Zealand in one test against New South Wales. Forty years later he represented New Zealand in bowls at the 1962 British Empire and Commonwealth Games in Perth.

The Christchurch Golf Club, founded in 1873, is New Zealand's second oldest golf club, and its Shirley course, opened in 1900, is still today one of the country's finest. Recent cosmetic changes under the direction of Australian legend and five-time British Open winner Peter Thomson have made the course more strategic, and improved its appearance.

Among the latest features are pot bunkers that give the place an old-world look, but the general layout remains much the same as it was when Mick Boon played here in the 1960s – and on the day when he scored what might be the most unlikely birdie on a par-5 hole.

The fourth hole, 'Lands End', is a banana-shaped par 5 about 450 metres long from the white tee. Although it now has more bunkers, it's not much longer than it was when Boon played it on that memorable day, if only because the club has never had more land to make it so.

The course is constrained in places by two paved roads. Lake Terrace Road cuts right through it, leaving eleven holes to play on one side,

info

The 4th
Par 5
450 metres

Christchurch Golf Club
45 Horseshoe Lake Road
Christchurch
Tel (03) 385 9506
www.christchurchgolf.co.nz

seven on the other. And then there's Horseshoe Lake Road, which runs alongside the 4th's fairway and provides some of the shape for the hole.

Mick Boon played golf right-handed. He teed off at the fourth and sliced his drive out over a fence and the out-of-bounds markers on to Horseshoe Lake Road. This would have been bad luck for Mick on any normal day, but to make it worse his ball struck a passing delivery van. It bounced off the vehicle and bounded back across the fence, coming to rest in the middle of the fairway.

Mick set up over his second shot, and struck it nicely enough to set up with a short third shot to the green, but he sculled the approach. The ball went sailing like a bullet over the green and out on to Lake Terrace Road, where it struck a passing car. The ball rebounded off the car and on to the green, coming to rest not far the pin – where, as cool as a wicketkeeper in the heat of the day, Boon knocked down the putt for a birdie.

The 18th at Avondale

KEITH FOXTON was a legend in Canterbury golf. He represented the province in ten inter-provincial championships in the 1950s and '60s, and was a member of three Canterbury teams that won the tournament.

Foxton reportedly had a sweet swing, and a short game worthy of Ripley's Believe It or Not! He was famous for chipping the ball into the hole from the most unlikely places. He was also a legendary drinker.

The 18th at the Avondale Golf Club is a par 3 about 175 metres long, and tight from tee to green. There are a few holes here where a right-handed player can get away with a slight fade, but the 18th isn't one of them. A fence line and out of bounds lie closely on the right all the way up to the green, while a pull to the left is nearly as useless.

After the first round of play in a two-day tournament here, Foxton had more than a few drinks. He was one of the last to leave the club and it was well after dark. Losing his bearings, he fell into the bunker at the 18th hole, where he slept the night off.

The next morning he got up, had a cup of tea, played the second round like a champion and won the tournament.

info

The 18th
Par 3
175 metres

Avondale Golf Club
Wainoni and Breezes Roads
Christchurch
Tel (03) 388 2675
www.avondalegolfclub.co.nz

The 2nd at Russley

THE BRISTOL FREIGHTER was a utility plane designed to carry British army trucks and heavy guns during the Second World War. After the war, it became a useful all-purpose cargo plane, popular enough for the Royal New Zealand Air Force to buy twelve of them.

By the late 1950s the air force was selling them off to private companies. One was bought by a company called Straits Air Freight Express. On Thursday, November 21, 1957, the SAFE plane made a run up from Timaru, via Woodbourne Aerodrome near Blenheim, to Paraparaumu, where it dropped off light cargo and one of its two passengers.

For the return run, Captain Robert Hamilton, first officer Harry Torgerson and SAFE general manager Tom O'Connell were joined by James McLaggen, a university student. The cargo? Two cows.

The second hole at the Russley Golf Club is called 'Nor'east' – appropriately so, because when that furious dry wind blows across the Canterbury Plains, this long and straight par 5, 465 metres from the back tee down a narrow fairway with trees flanking both sides, leaves many players happy enough scoring bogey.

This could be a signature hole of Russley. It's a perfect example of what one member said was the best way to play the course: 'Hit the bloody ball down the middle.'

The Bristol Freighter was flying at about 900 metres when it passed over the control tower at Harewood Airport (now Christchurch International), beginning its descent to Timaru. A strong nor'easter was causing severe turbulence and tossing the plane about. Just seconds after the captain reported in at Harwood, the plane's starboard wing folded up and back and then fell off. The plane dropped sharply, and just before impact more parts of its body broke away, scattering for more than a mile.

As the rest of the plane nosedived into pine trees on Russley Golf Course's south-east boundary and exploded in a sheet of flame, debris landed on the fairway of the second hole. It was later reported that some golfers, unaware of the disaster, were annoyed at their game being disrupted by the heavy vehicles that rumbled over the course to the scene.

James McLaggen survived the crash, but died on the golf course before help could arrive. Captain Hamilton, his first officer and the company boss were incinerated in the ball of fire. One of the blackened cows was left dangling from a branch in a burnt-out tree.

On November 21, 2007, to mark the fiftieth anniversary of the tragedy, a permanent memorial was placed at the hole.

info

The 2nd
Par 5
465 metres

Russley Golf Club
428 Memorial Avenue
Christchurch
Tel (03) 358 4612
www.russleygolfclub.co.nz

The 11th at Templeton

DON HOPE is known today as one of New Zealand's most successful magazine publishers. In the early 1980s, he co-founded *Fashion Quarterly*, a magazine that did much to set in motion the country's home-grown fashion industry, which has gone from strength to strength and is today attracting world attention.

Hope's latest magnum opus, *World* magazine, is a publication well suited to an emergent demographic of New Zealanders who, when they were growing up in the 1960s, never dreamed of being as well off and worldly as they are now. He describes it as showcasing the best the world has to offer in fashion, design, art, gourmet food and wine, and travel.

In the '60s Hope was among the most talented young golfers in the land. He has a quick backswing, like the Australian legend Ted Ball. A quick backswing suggests an uncompromising commitment to striking the ball and it was this that led Hope to win the Canterbury Under-17, Under-21 and Open championships.

The 11th hole at the Templeton Golf Club, like any golf hole rendered as a diagram on a scorecard, is straight and narrow, even mundane and ho-hum. It's a 468-metre par 5 from the tips, with a gully on the right. The fairway jumps around somewhat, because the course is laid out on land shaped over time by the ebb and flow of the Waimakariri River.

In that way, this golf course has more character than its scorecard suggests, and a shot by Don Hope at the 11th in 1967 to win the

Canterbury Open is a sampling of that. Hope has called it 'the greatest shot of my life'.

He was twenty-one years old and up against a veteran named Toby Richards in match play for the title. Richards, a farmer from Hororata, was a highly respected player. He and Hope had both been members of the Canterbury team that had won the Freyberg Rose Bowl in 1965.

Hope's tee shot at the 11th came to rest in the fairway all right, but lying in someone's divot. Striking a golf ball cleanly out of a small hole in the ground, with no grass for the club to bounce off, is a trick in itself, but using a two-iron Hope dug the ball out of the dirt and drove it far enough to reach the green in two. It came to a stop just three feet from the pin and he made the putt for an eagle.

Why do we play golf? One answer is to make at least one good shot, maybe even a great one – a shot that becomes a cherished memory – because more often than not the story of a single shot stays fresh longer than the score on the day.

Don Hope gave up competitive golf after a few years, but his love of the game led him to found another international magazine, *Golf, Leisure & Lifestyle*, in 1995.

info

The 11th
Par 5
468 metres

Templeton Golf Club
Pound Road
Christchurch
Tel (03) 349 7493
www.templetongc.co.nz

The 3rd at Akaroa

THERE'S AN OLD SAYING: If you can't go to France, go to Akaroa. Actually that's not an old saying: I just made it up, but with good reason.

Banks Peninsula was known to the local iwi, Ngai Tahu, as Horomaka until Captain James Cook mapped it out in 1769, naming it for Joseph Banks, his much esteemed botanist on the *Endeavour*.

The following century saw English exploration evolve into settlement in the Bay of Islands and elsewhere, leading in 1840 to the signing of the Treaty of Waitangi, wherein most Maori, if not all, accepted the Queen of England as the Queen of Aotearoa.

Whether or not this was a big mistake for Maori, it did keep the French out. No sooner had the treaty been signed than a ship carrying French settlers turned up in Pigeon Bay on the north coast of Banks Peninsula, aiming to claim the South Island for France.

Sorry, no vacancy. The British had already whipped down here and planted the Union Jack.

That was all there was to the attempted French takeover of Aotearoa but it was enough to establish a tourism industry. Akaroa is today New Zealand's 'Petite France' and the annual Akaroa French Fest in October is a bigger celebration than ever.

Enjoy a taste of faux France, hire a four-wheel drive to see penguins and seals, have a peek in the Okains Bay Maori and Colonial Museum – these are all fine things to do. But if getting off the tourism trail is what you're after, play golf.

The third hole at the Akaroa Golf Club is a steep climb, but the view of the harbour may prove to be better than your putting. The hole is a par 3 about 120 metres long for men and just over 100 metres for women, but it plays up a slope that will play with you more than you play with it. It's a test of mind against body, and mind wins most of the time.

info

The 3rd
Par 3
120 metres

Akaroa Golf Club
Pawsons Valley Road
Duvauchelle, Akaroa
Tel (03) 304 5704
akaroagolf@paradise.net.nz

The green is a raised plateau that falls away on all sides, most noteworthily on the left where, if you miss, your ball will more than likely disappear down a steep embankment and come to rest, finally, on the second fairway, from where your caddy may say, 'Je vous attends ici' ('I will wait for you here').

The 16th at Terrace Downs

THE GOVERNMENT HAS A HISTORY of honouring veterans, and after the Second World War, to honour the men who had put their life on the line overseas, it handed out freehold land. Edwin Tilley won a parcel at the foot of Mount Hutt, overlooking the Rakaia Gorge. Seeing the way the land, carved out by the river, had formed terraces, he called his farm Terrace Downs.

In 1990 Tilley sold the farm to a professional golfer from Japan named Shinnosuke Saito. As you might expect a professional golfer to do, Saito converted it into a golf resort. The golf course was designed by the Canadian firm of Puddicombe Golf, landscape design specialists known for their good work elsewhere in New Zealand.

Today, Terrace Downs has settled into a fine high-country golf course like no other in the country, because it sits at the foot of the mighty Mount Hutt Range and looks over the Rakaia River and Gorge. And it's the gorge that makes the par-3 sixteenth hole the star of the show.

This is a short hole even by par-3 standards. From the tee it appears close enough to reach out and touch. Yet, because it's perched on the edge of a cliff that drops straight down to the river, scoring par here requires more steel, as in nerves of steel, than iron, however long or short.

There are a number of noteworthy scenic golf holes in New Zealand and many of them are par 3s, but this is one that can take your breath

away – and note, if you are not breathing normally you will probably not strike the ball as well as you should.

The green slopes from back to front. It has a bunker on the left and one in front. If you miss on the right – or as is all too common, you strike a weak-kneed shot that comes up short – do *not* venture over the side looking for your ball.

info

The 16th
Par 3
100 metres

Terrace Downs
Coleridge Road
Windwhistle
Tel (03) 317 9370
www.terracedowns.co.nz

In 2007 Shinnosuke Saito sold Terrace Downs to two New Zealand investors, who are aiming to expand the experiences on offer to include equestrian sports, archery and clay pigeon shooting. Whether that happens remains to be seen, but one thing is sure: the 16th hole will remain one of golf's most heart-stopping experiences.

The 8th at Greymouth

PETER MCGEE IS A LEFTIE – that is, he is a left-handed golfer like, for instance, Bob Charles. It is not recorded if Peter McGee and Bob Charles ever played together but it's not a far-fetched notion because McGee is a member of the Greymouth Golf Club and Sir Bob has played here in both tournament and charity golf. In fact he has declared the 329-metre par-4 eighth hole one of the finest holes in New Zealand.

The hole is called 'Ellery's' for long-time club member Neil Ellery, who once scored a 17 on it. It has a two-tiered fairway that turns sharply left. From the turn it is only 135 metres to the green, but because there are two trees on the fairway it can require something like a trick shot in order to reach it. Players try to avoid the trees, but it is as if they move: no matter how hard you try to place the ball around them, they commonly end up in the direct path to the pin. Take a short iron and loft the ball over them, or punch a long iron under them – it's your call.

Nonetheless, like Bob Charles, Peter McGee may think this is one of the finest holes in New Zealand golf because it was here that he scored what could be recorded as the greatest par ever scored on a par-4 hole – anywhere, any time, any place.

Greymouth has a rich history of well-known professionals appearing – golfing greats John Lister and Simon Owen, Australian legend Roger Davis and Englishman Maurice Bembridge have all played here – but I doubt any of them scored par on the 8th like Peter McGee did one day.

McGee, the leftie, tees off on the 8th and slices his drive, which means it curls sharply right to left. The ball appears to be headed over the fence, into trees, out of bounds. But it strikes a tree fair and square, and ricochets back out into the fairway.

McGee then slices his second shot. This sails right to left and, like his tee shot, appears to be headed into the great unknown when it too strikes a tree and ricochets back into the fairway.

info

The 8th
Par 4
329 metres

Greymouth Golf Club
Golf Links Road
Kaiata
Greymouth
Tel (03) 768 5332
www.greymouthgolf.synthasite.com

With his third shot – and by now he's not very far from the green – he again cuts across the ball with the face of his club and slices it, and again it pops back out off a tree. The ball ends up just off the green, from where McGee chips in for par.

The 14th at Hokitika

MEMBERS OF THE HOKITIKA GOLF CLUB fondly recall the penguin. It was never given a name. Known simply as 'the penguin', it kept a nest under the bar of the clubhouse. It was cute at first, but in time it created a horrible stink and had to be removed. One story has it that members lifted it out, put it up on the bar, and raised their glasses to the dumbfounded bird, before it was taken away to live in peace further down the coast.

This was life on the West Coast as it was experienced by Arnold James Thompson. Thompson, born in 1904, did not begin playing golf until he was in his thirties, but he took to it with the determination of a West Coast westerly. The wind can be fierce here, and because the Hokitika Golf Club, a hidden gem, is just off the beach you can smell the salty sea air from any hole on the course.

Here on the West Coast it's easy enough to imagine that someone as hooked on golf as Arnold Thompson would have played through the toughest conditions imaginable. His devotion to the game and the club was such that the 14th hole is called 'Thompson's Corner'. A 330-metre par 4, it has a hump down the middle of the fairway that makes keeping the ball in play as much a matter of luck as skill.

Over time Arnold Thompson's son, Michael, took up golf. Michael Thompson learned the game from his father, and like his father was – and still is – a loyal club member. Michael played the game exception-

ally well: in one thirty-year stretch he won the men's club championship twenty-four times.

Michael then taught his son Stuart to play the game, and as oedipal as it sounds, when Michael failed to win the club championship it was because of Stuart. The 14th at Hokitika, 'Thompson's Corner', is the only golf hole in the country named for three generations of players. In a natural progression, Stuart, now the popular club professional at The Grange Golf Club in Auckland, turned pro and in 1999 he won the Tahitian Open. By the way, a new clubhouse has been built since the days of the penguin.

info

The 14th
Par 4
330 metres

Hokitika Golf Club
Golf Links Road
Hokitika
Tel (03) 755 8549
hokitika@golf.co.nz

The 10th at St Andrews

MOST GOLF PUNDITS, including America's *Golf Digest*, consider the Old Course at St Andrews in Scotland the crème de la crème of golf courses. It is also the most historic. Golf is said to have been invented there six centuries ago, when fishermen got into the sport of trying to hit pebbles on the beach into rabbit holes. Not everyone was keen on the idea. In 1457 the Scottish parliament passed an act banning 'gowfe' as it was getting in the way of soldiers practising archery. Fifty years later, when Scotland signed a peace agreement with England and the arrows were back in their quivers, at least temporarily, James IV commissioned a set of golf clubs, and life as we golfers know it began.

Let's be clear, the St Andrews Golf Club in Canterbury, New Zealand and the one in Scotland are not related. When the Canterbury club was formed in the mid 1970s, the founders wrote to the Royal and Ancient Golf Club of St Andrews to gain permission to use the name; after all, the name of the district in Canterbury, south of Timaru, where the golf course would be located was called St Andrews. In return, the R&AGC sent them a magazine subscription form.

The Canterbury St Andrews declined to subscribe, and nothing more has been said about the common name since – until now, of course. And lest people in Waikato take umbrage, let me also note that there is an even older St Andrews Golf Course in Hamilton.

As if you haven't guessed already, the Canterbury district of St Andrews was settled by Scottish immigrants. Among their descendants was Noel Galletly, who farmed the land that is today the golf club. Noel did not play golf but his daughter Glenda did. Glenda was in her twenties, married with children, when a neighbour suggested she give golf a go and she hasn't stopped playing since. Glenda Hardacre, as she is today, plays at least once a week on a 23 handicap.

One day Noel decided to give up farming, which meant he had to make a decision about what to do with the land. Because his daughter enjoyed playing golf so much, he sold it at mate's rates to a group who wanted to form a club in the neighbourhood. Until then, the closest course where Glenda and her friends could play was a nine-hole track on the lower slopes of the Hunter Hills at Maungati.

The 10th hole at St Andrews, aptly named 'Noel', is a long par 4 for men, a short par 5 for women. The fairway bends slightly from right to left, and while there are no bunkers to hold anyone up, putting can be interesting because of the split-level green.

This was the original first hole but not long ago the club renumbered the holes. The front nine became the back and the back nine became the front, which is too bad because 'Noel' was the perfect opening hole – long but friendly to the point where even a high handicapper such as Glenda could score a birdie on it – which is what she did one day.

info

The 10th
Par 4
379 metres

St Andrews Golf Club
State Highway One
St Andrews
Tel (03) 612 6590
www.standrewsgolfclub.co.nz

The 17th at North Otago

THE EARLY HISTORY OF GOLF in New Zealand in the 1890s is firmly associated with clubs such as Otago, Christchurch and Hutt, but one club often forgotten from that era is North Otago.

In part this may be because it is in Oamaru. Blame it on New Zealand's world-famous novelist Janet Frame if you wish, but Oamaru, where Frame lived as a girl and which features in some of her books, is sometimes perceived as a dark and mysterious place. It is not, like Taupo or Queenstown, a holiday town, even though it has a terrific collection of Victorian and neoclassical buildings. The Opera House is especially cool.

The North Otago Golf Club was one of the original four 'senior' clubs that chipped in to purchase the Amateur Cup, the trophy presented to the winner of the New Zealand men's amateur championship. There is as much history of the game here, in other words, as there is at Otago, Christchurch and Hutt.

The best sea view is from the top of this hilly course. It's a climb, but if you're knocking a golf ball about the climb may be the last thing on your mind. That's the joy of golf: it demands so much concentration you forget about everything else, even if you're out of breath. And here a southerly means that even in summer, with sunshine and clear blue skies, you can still nearly freeze to death if you don't have the proper gear.

The 17th hole, 'Waterloo', is a par 3 that is 145 metres long for men, 110 metres for women. It plays downhill from an elevated tee. The hole

is nicely framed by a row of poplar trees on one side and bluegums on the other, and the trick is to avoid the bunkers surrounding one of the longest greens – 48 metres – in the South Island.

info

The 17th
Par 3
145 metres

North Otago Golf Club
Beach Road
Oamaru
Tel (03) 434 5531
www.nzgolfcourses.co.nz/northotago/club.htm

The book *Golf in New Zealand: A Centennial History* notes that in 1927, after the mayor of Oamaru had officially opened this course, 'Further ceremonies of baptism followed when R.G. Mathieson holed out at Waterloo'. The feat, in those times, was more handsomely rewarded than today. Mr Mathieson qualified for the Valet Hole-in-One Club, which entitled him to a 25-shilling Valet Autostrop Shaving Set Deluxe. Dewars' Cordial Manufacturing Company also contributed a bottle of health restorer.

You see, there are surprises in life, even in Oamaru.

The 11th at Balmacewen

IN 1863 THE *OTAGO WITNESS* ran an advertisement calling for a meeting of 'Gentleman desirous of forming a golf club'. Dunedin in those days had few gentlemen and not many of them were interested in golf, so it was another six years before Charles Ritchie Howden, the man who placed the ad, found someone to play with. Two years later the Dunedin Golf Club was formed and, like a good Scot, Howden named himself club captain.

He and his mates cut nine greens out of a cow paddock. The farmer, obviously not a golfer, wouldn't allow the club to fence off their greens, so cows tramped mindlessly over the new 'holes', not knowing they were destroying a man-made sporting venue handed down from God.

The farmer eventually went broke. He sold the farm to someone who wasn't at all keen on having his cows run the risk of getting clobbered by a golf ball, so it was another twenty years before golf was played in a regular way again in New Zealand, when a still determined Charles Ritchie Howden and others formed the Otago Golf Club in 1892.

The club thrived without attracting much attention until 1935, when the great Gene Sarazen, holder of one British Open, two United States Opens, and four PGA Championships, turned up. He was the first international golf celebrity to play in New Zealand and it set a pattern of inviting some of the world's finest players to play at Balmacewen.

That's how Arnold Palmer came to be here in 1966. Palmer was then

one of the longest off the tee in all of golf. He dazzled a large gallery, including some who had never seen golf played before, with his long drives, so there was high expectation when he moved to the 11th tee.

info

The 11th
Par 4
300 metres
Otago Golf Club
125 Balmacewen Road
Dunedin
Tel (03) 467 2096
www.otagogolfclub.co.nz

The eleventh at Balmacewen has one of the most elevated tees in relation to the green in New Zealand. However, the hole is only 300 metres long, which means that from the very high tee it is driveable. And The King drove the green.

Driving the green at 'The Glenn', as the hole is called, is not uncommon today, but the green is long and slopes steadily from front to back so even being there in one doesn't guarantee a 2-putt for a birdie. An embarrassing, deflating 3-putt is common. Worse, if the tee shot is too long the ball can easily fly into Ross Creek Reserve at the back.

Arnold Palmer drove the ball deep, but not quite that far. Still, he was faced with a long putt simply to get close to the hole and have a chance of making par. His gallery of fans – Arnie's Army – was nervous as he stepped up. Surely he wouldn't 3-putt? Luckily The King left his first putt close enough to the hole to sink the second for a birdie.

The 9th at Chisholm Park

LAID OUT ACROSS Dunedin's cliff-topped coastline, the ninth hole at the Chisholm Park Golf Club may have the most unnerving tee you'll ever stand on. It sits only a few feet from the edge of a cliff that drops forty metres or more straight down. Pros have been known to be so spooked by it that it affects their swing. And when there's money on the line the last place they want a shot to end up is down below on Tomahawk Beach.

Chisholm Park is a coastal gem of a golf course and the ninth hole, a par 4 that not only plays from a precarious tee up to a plateau fairway but then over two gullies to a kidney-shaped green, is great fun. Because of its location, misjudge an approach shot here and what looks at first to be a spot-on shot can bounce once or twice on the green before disappearing over the back edge.

With Tomahawk Beach to the north and St Clair Beach to the south, the views on a fine day from up here are worth checking out, even if you eschew golf. If nothing else, bring a putter and have a go on the ninth green when no one is watching. Keep an eye out for sea lions basking in the sun below.

Wind is always a factor of course, and here the decision to play or not is a measure of one's sanity. Just as there are surfers who can't wait for a good blast from the south, there are golf crazies who eagerly await the chance to play this hole into a wicked southerly, just for the thrill.

On those longed-for days they watch as their tee shot boomerangs back over their head.

Contrary to what you might think, the club's popular professional, Andrew Whiley, says high winds are more a factor here in the summer months than winter. Who would have thought that the best time to play this Dunedin course and its famous ninth hole might be July or August?

info

The 9th
Par 4
353 metres

Chisholm Park Golf Club
16 Tahuna Road
Dunedin
Tel (03) 455 0565
www.chisholmlinks.co.nz

The 15th at St Clair

AMERICAN JOHNNY MILLER turned up at the St Clair Golf Club in 1972 to play in the Otago Charity Classic, a professional tournament held here each year from 1970 to 1979. The tournament attracted major international stars and helped spawn the careers of New Zealand players.

Miller grew up in San Francisco, where he learned to play golf at the Olympic Golf Club, a prestigious private club and the site of a number of important championships, including the United States Open. The year he appeared here he was known as a rising star who had finished eighth at the 1966 US Open as a nineteen-year-old amateur.

So he flies all the way down to New Zealand and further down to Dunedin and turns up at St Clair, where he's paired with a local hotshot named Nick Smith. Smith is one of the top amateurs in Otago and drives the ball a proverbial mile. Smith is competing with Miller shot for shot when they arrive at the 15th tee, where, it seems, Miller has had just about enough of the challenge from the local amateur.

The par-4 fifteenth at St Clair is one of New Zealand's great golf holes, if only for its tee that doubles as a viewing platform for one of the most sensational coastal views you can imagine, stretching to the Black Head peninsula and beyond. The mock AA signpost next to the tee points the way to the South Pole, just 4,913 kilometres away. The green, meanwhile, is about 350 metres away.

A slight southerly is coming in, so at the 15th hole players have the wind at their back. As if to show the young American what he can do, Smith turns the competition into a long driver contest and drives his ball up close to the green. In reply, Miller drives his ball *over* the green.

Johnny Miller won the Otago Charity Classic. The following year he won the United States Open with a final round 63 that is considered one of the greatest final rounds in the history of the game. He began the day six shots back of the four greatest players of the time – Nicklaus, Palmer, Player and Trevino – and beat them all. By then he had probably forgotten altogether the name of the guy who tried to steal his thunder at St Clair.

info

The 15th
Par 4
350 metres

St Clair Golf Club
20 Isadore Road
Dunedin
Tel (03) 487 7076
www.stclairgolf.co.nz

The 11th at Cromwell

A FEW YEARS AGO one of New Zealand's most successful professionals, Greg Turner, a multiple winner on the European Tour who is today a golf course design consultant, changed the 11th at the Cromwell Golf Club from a straight, narrow and rather ordinary hole into an interesting dog-leg. The change made perfect sense, because the hole is named for a dog.

Sailor is one of the most famous dogs in New Zealand golf – even if a lot of people outside of Cromwell have never heard of him. For club members, he was more than just a fondly remembered cocker spaniel: he was a legend akin to Lassie.

Sailor was the loyal companion of Ken Munro. Munro was born on a farm near Tarras in Central Otago in 1878. After years working on a sheep farm and rabbiting, Munro retired to Cromwell in the 1950s and became the volunteer greenkeeper of the Cromwell Golf Club.

One day, while Munro and Sailor were making the rounds, the dog disappeared into tall grass, only to reappear again proudly carrying a golf ball in his mouth. Sailor, it turned out, could smell a golf ball like no dog people had known before. It's been said that on one particular day he found more than a hundred, most of them Top-Flite or Dunlop, the two major brands of the time, and most of them presumably lost.

Ken Munro was quick to identify Sailor's extraordinary talent as a commercial opportunity. He asked golfers to initial their balls. If they

lost one, the dog would find it and the golfer would pay a one-shilling 'search fee' to club coffers. One year, according to the club's annual report, the dog's contribution totalled twenty pounds and fifteen shillings.

'Sailor', as the eleventh at Cromwell is called today, is perfectly suited for players who fade the ball. It's a blind tee shot, so most visitors will think that by hitting straight up the middle they are playing it safe. But because of the dog-leg, a tee shot that is too long and straight can run through the turn into rough, and maybe even under a grove of fine birch trees.

Sailor will not be finding your ball. He passed away from natural causes in 1957. Ken Munro was ninety-five when he followed in 1973.

info

The 11th
Par 4
322 metres

Cromwell Golf Club
Neplusultra Street
Cromwell
Tel (03) 445 0165
www.cromwellgolf.co.nz

The 13th at Arrowtown

IF SOMEONE WERE EVER TO ORGANISE a referendum on New Zealand's most charming town, my guess is that Arrowtown would win. What is it about old mining towns? Maybe it's the mountains and mountain air more than the town, for there are plenty of nineteenth-century buildings dripping with charm elsewhere too. But there's something about the story of gold that is especially alluring and, unlike mining coal, panning for gold was relatively easy and clean – so much so it's fun for the whole family today. Hire a pan ($5) and give it a go. There's a stream just across the street from Saffron, the best restaurant in town.

info

The 13th
Par 5
459 metres

Arrowtown Golf Club
166 Centennial Avenue
Arrowtown
Tel (03) 442 1719
www.arrowtowngolf.co.nz

The Arrowtown Golf Club is a minute's drive north of town, but it is easy to miss because it blends so well with the landscape, one accentuated by stark peaks and a rugged, hearty countryside that looks especially dramatic because of its schist outcrops – the singular feature that gives this course its character.

Arrowtown has no bunkers, but it doesn't need them because its hazards – big rocks – can be more punishing than sand. Have you ever seen a golf ball ricochet off a rock?

The schist outcrops make this golf course special. The jeweller Michael Hill has a few on his ultra-private course, The Hills, just down the road, but you won't see them unless he invites you to play. This course and its architecturally award-winning clubhouse opened in 2007. Arrowtown is not as flash as The Hills but it has more personality. The elevated ninth tee is the best observation point for an overview, one that includes Coronet Peak and the Crown Range.

The 13th hole is a 459-metre par 5 framed by rocks, yet finishing with a poet's touch. The fairway is straight, more or less, so there are no tricks to scoring par here, apart from striking a good tee shot, followed by a solid and straight fairway wood. The third shot will hopefully avoid two cherry trees that guard the green like royal guards outside Kensington Palace. Greenkeeper Rick Machray says the best time to catch these Peggy Wilson cherry trees in full bloom, their soft pink flowers lighting up the 13th green like neon, is in late September or early October.

The 18th at Arrowtown

FOR ALL THE ROCKS and schist outcrops and massive mountain peaks that shape the character of this town and its golf course, the closing hole at Arrowtown is a great, and often deeply troublesome, hole because of water, not stone.

The hole is called 'Lady Fayre' after one of the numerous gold mines that operated in this area from the early 1860s. Few, if any, of the miners made their fortunes; most lived miserable lives, especially in the snow-ridden winters. The remains of one of their settlements, Macetown, have recently been faithfully restored, and if you travel by four-wheel drive over twenty-two fords in the Arrow River, you can visit Anderson's all-metal stamping battery, Needham's Cottage, Smith's Bakehouse, and even some original fruit trees.

The ghostly goldminers of Lady Fayre haunt the 18th hole – the elevated green of which slopes severely right to left towards a pond – taking their revenge on every naïve hack who comes along thinking that, after a steady seventeen holes and a fine round, the 18th will be a mere formality.

Unfortunately, they push their final tee shot of the day too far right. Un-

Arrowtown cottages

able to fade the ball around and up to the elevated green, they pull the second shot too far left… and watch as it disappears into the pond.

It doesn't stop there. The fourth shot is short and left. It bounces off the steep bank by the green and rolls into the pond. Overcompensating, the sixth shot is too far right and long. It lands above the green and rolls off the back. The seventh shot, a chip shot, catches the down slope and rolls off the green into rough. The ninth shot, alas, stays on the green, where the victim two-putts for an eleven and the miners of Lady Fayre laugh in their graves.

info

The 18th
Par 4
324 metres

Arrowtown Golf Club
166 Centennial Avenue
Arrowtown
Tel (03) 442 1719
www.arrowtowngolf.co.nz

The 18th at Arrowtown is 324 metres long – average length for a par 4 – but its shape, the position of the pond and the height and slope of the green are a spirited combination that can leave you spooked for days afterwards.

The 18th at Millbrook

MILLBROOK, the first true golf resort in the country – where resort means a championship quality golf course plus all the trimmings – restaurant and bar, luxurious accommodation, tennis courts, indoor swimming pool, gym and spa – opened to much acclaim in the early 1990s.

Golf resorts can look and sound sensational, but managing them in a way that makes money is not easy. Golf resorts are like movies: just because they are made doesn't mean they are good. But Millbrook has not only survived, it has grown better with age.

As a measure of that, when New Zealand hosted the Asia-Pacific Economic Development (APEC) summit in 1999, Millbrook was part of the itinerary. It was the perfect place to take a group of overseas guests to experience some of the best Central Otago has to offer, foremost the mountains, the wine – especially the famed pinot noir – and the golf. The last was especially important because United States president Bill Clinton was a golfer.

Burton Shipley, husband of the prime minister, Jenny Shipley, who was hosting the APEC meeting, played with Clinton that day. In an email to me, he revealed: 'All the way around we had a challenge to keep the cart going reasonably slowly with the two of us in it. The president told me, "They don't let me drive much, so I like to drive on the golf course".'

The 18th is a par 5, and about 500 metres long from the back tee. It plays downhill to a green with a stream flowing directly in front of it. It is framed by trees and a café and bar, making it altogether one of the most delicious and welcoming finishing holes in New Zealand.

info

The 18th
Par 5
505 metres

Millbrook Resort
Malaghans Road
Arrowtown
Tel (03) 441 7010
www.millbrook.co.nz

By all accounts Bill Clinton had a swell time. The weather was perfect, The Remarkables mountain range stood tall in all its glory against an azure sky, and the president, showing his genius for meeting and greeting people along the way, enjoyed playing the 18th hole so much he played it twice.

The 5th at Kelvin Heights

ONE FINE DAY, while I was standing on the tee of the par-4 fifth hole at the Queenstown Golf Club, the group in front was especially slow, so I had time to turn around and take a long solid look at the shark-tooth peaks of The Remarkables high above.

Later, my amateur interest in geology had me online trying to learn more about that ultra-dramatic mountain range, one of the two majestic features that make this hole a must. In the *New Zealand Journal*

info

The 5th
Par 4
362 metres

Queenstown Golf Club
Peninsula Road
Kelvin Heights
Queenstown
Tel (03) 442 9169
www.queenstowngolf.co.nz

of Geology and Geophysics, Simon Cox, a geologist at the University of Otago had written: 'At the northern end of The Remarkables … psammitic schists of the Caples terrane pass downwards through a 300-metre thick transitional zone into pelitic schists of the Aspiring terrane.'

Hey, everyone knows that.

The second feature that makes this hole special is that it plays along and around the shoreline of Lake Wakatipu, the only water hazard in New Zealand golf where, from the tee, you can see heads with snorkel masks and breathing pipes bobbing in the water, waiting like vultures for someone to pull their tee shot into the lake. Sure, you can get that new $10 ball back, for $10.

The hole plays around and somewhat uphill to a two-tiered green, where, even if you reach the green in two, two-putting for par, to say nothing of scoring a birdie, is still a feat. The problem is a lack of concentration, caused first by the mountain spectacle above, then by the shimmering lake – and, from the green, The Remarkables and those intriguing psammitic and pelitic schists.

The 10th at Kelvin Heights

THE RECORD DOESN'T SHOW whether Sam Lee woke up on New Year's Day 2008 with a hangover. We do know, though, that he headed out for a round of golf at the Queenstown Golf Club's Kelvin Heights course, and that in the middle of the morning he struck a fine tee shot at the tenth – one of the most picturesque golf holes imaginable.

The distance from tee to green at this par-3 hole is only 110 metres. The hole plays even shorter than that because the tee is higher than the green. Even though there's a water hazard on the left, the distance is so short the pond is not intimidating. In fact, this is the No. 18 stroke hole, the 'easiest' on the course. If there is a degree of difficulty, it is keeping your focus on the task at hand, rather than on the cinematic backdrop of the lake and Walter Peak.

The 10th calls for a short iron for men, a middle iron for women. Sam Lee used a wedge. The ball flew directly at the hole and bounced a couple times on the green, before rolling straight into the cup. At eleven o'clock in the morning, Lee had scored the year's first hole-in-one in the world.

info

The 10th
Par 3
110 metres

Queenstown Golf Club
Peninsula Road
Kelvin Heights
Queenstown
Tel (03) 442 9169
www.queenstowngolf.co.nz

The 8th at Jack's Point

IN THE WINTER OF 1862, a man known as Maori Jack was ferrying a boat on Lake Wakatipu with two other men – a run-holder, William Rogers, and an English visitor, John Mitchell – when a sudden squall came up and the boat capsized. As anyone who's been to Queenstown knows, the water in Lake Wakatipu is brutally cold, even in summer, so the thought of winding up in that lake in the middle of winter is enough to shiver the spine.

info

The 8th
Par 5
480 metres

Jack's Point Golf Club
State Highway Six
Queenstown
Tel (03) 450 2050
www.jackspoint.com

Given the cold, the men did not have long to live unless they could reach shore. The problem was the boat had overturned and was filling with water, about to sink. Incredibly, Jack found the will and strength to flip the boat upright and get Mitchell back in, then swim to shore pulling the boat behind him. Unfortunately, he was not able to rescue Rogers, who had been swept away.

As if this extraordinary story needed a sub-theme, after Jack had got John Mitchell to shore, a dog that had been missing for many years appeared from the bush and lay next to the half-drowned man, keeping him warm while Jack ran to find help.

For his life-saving courage Jack was awarded a medal by the Royal Humane Society of Britain. In 2006 this medal was given to the Lakes District Museum in nearby Arrowtown and you can see it there.

The following year, Jack, whose real name was Jack Tewa, went on to be the first person to discover gold in the Arrow River, and thereby started a gold rush that transformed Central Otago.

The new golf course near the site of this incident is named for him. Designed by John Darby, Jack's Point is a stunner. And although it carries a degree of difficulty comparable to Kinloch (see page 126), the lake and mountains – the course sits at the foot of The Remarkables and in view of Walter Peak – make this a captivating place to play.

The par-5 eighth hole plays along the lake, close to the actual site of Jack Tewa's famous rescue. Clear the fairway bunkers on the left and it's uphill to a 'blind' green.

The 10th at Te Anau

HAVE YOU NEVER SCORED an eagle on a par 5? Here's your chance.

The 10th hole at the Te Anau Golf Club is a par 5 that is only 386 metres long – and that's from the back tee. Given the twenty-first century super-substances now used to make golf balls and clubs, there is no doubt someone out there who can reach this green in one blow. Perhaps there is even someone with the ability to do what no person has ever done in the history of the game to the best of my knowledge: score a hole-in-one on a par 5.

Of course, there's a catch. The raised green, a small hill with its nose cut off, drops away sharply on both sides and out the back. The entry is cut narrow, so the chances of rolling the ball on to the green with a tee shot, or even the second shot for that matter, are small. Miss the green to the right and you can lose the ball altogether down a steep bank of tall grass.

This may be the shortest par-5 hole in the world for all I know, but as gorgeous as this course is on a perfect day – when Lake Te Anau, the Murchison Range and Mount Luxmore, the inner edge of Fiordland National Park, can be seen from every hole – the heart-stopping beauty is often lost on those who lose their balls.

As Dawn Dowling, a club member who had taken her love of golf to the next level by building Dock Bay Lodge on the 11th fairway, reminded me: if it's the entire sweep of autumn colours you're after, April is

the best month to play here. That said, the 10th is the kind of hole that can make you feel good about yourself all year round.

Te Anau is also the stepping off point for the famous and incomparable Milford Track, a four-day walk, and near the start of the beautiful three-day Routeburn Track. If you are about to go tramping, take the time to limber up on this lovely golf course.

info

The 10th
Par 5
386 metres

Te Anau Golf Club
164 Golf Course Road
Te Anau
Tel (03) 249 7474
teanau@paradise.net.nz

The 14th at Otatara

EUGENIO SARACENI was born in 1902, the son of Italian immigrants in upstate New York. Look what a name change can do for some people. He changed his name to Gene Sarazen and became one of the greatest golfers who ever lived.

Sarazen was most famous for the 'shot heard round the world' – his second shot on the par-5 fifteenth hole on the final day of the 1935 Masters at Augusta. Using a four-wood he knocked his second shot in the hole, scoring perhaps the most famous albatross in the history of the game, and came from three shots down to win the tournament.

Sarazen arrived in New Zealand in 1936, and made it all the way down to Invercargill to play at Otatara, a course he described as having the best fairways of any he played in New Zealand. No doubt one of the fairways he was talking about was the 14th – the No. 2 stroke hole. This is a 412-metre par 4 and the sharpest dog-leg on the course, with out of bounds down the left. The bend where the hole turns right is known as Tatters Corner, after a dog who had such a knack for finding lost golf balls the club made him a life member in 1949.

info

The 14th
Par 4
412 metres

Invercargill Golf Club
190 Dunns Road
Invercargill
Tel (03) 213 1133
www.invercargillgolf.co.nz

The 11th at Oreti Sands

IF YOU CAN'T OPEN FIFTY OYSTERS in less than three minutes, forget it. If you can't stuff a dozen oysters in your mouth in less than ten seconds using a toothpick, forget it. Those are the kinds of numbers and times required to have any chance at all of winning the shellfish contests at the Bluff Oyster and Food Festival.

Better you try to win the Oyster Sack Fashion competition instead.

If there's a good reason to go to Bluff it must be this annual festival, and while you're there you may feel like a game of golf too.

Sadly, by the standards set for this book I am unable to include a hole from the golf course at Bluff, even if it is the self-proclaimed most southern golf course in New Zealand. Bluff is a nine-holer rough-cut from farm paddock – nothing more, nothing less.

If you're looking for something more and one round is all you have time for, play Oreti Sands, formally known as the Southland Golf Club. This course is located at the far end of a dedicated recreation park with sites for just about every sport that people play in Southland, including golf. Should you live in Invercargill and wish to take up archery, you know where to go.

Four new holes designed by Greg Turner and Scott Macpherson of Turner Macpherson Golf Design are due to open at Oreti Sands in 2009. The golf course is only a few sand dunes away from Oreti Beach and Foveaux Strait, so you can imagine how four new holes designed by

people who know what they're doing may turn around the fortunes of this rustic but forgotten links.

Play a round here and, assuming the committee is continuing the practice, they will give you a certificate for playing the southernmost 18-hole golf course in the world.

If nothing else, the second green is noteworthy because of its severe slope and the fact that it is large enough to stage a Broadway musical on.

Yet, if there's an essential hole at Oreti Sands it is the par-4 eleventh, a hole with a blind tee shot – that is, the green is not visible from the tee – and framed nicely by dunes and pines that neatly express the fundamental character of the course. I managed to find the fairway with the tee shot, but then pushed the second shot over a dune and into a grove of pines before three-putting for a double bogey.

I regret not going back to the eleventh tee and playing the hole again. After all, this was Southland on a midweek day in March, and if there was anyone else on the course I didn't see them.

In 2006, the magazine *Travel+ Leisure Golf* included Oreti Sands in its list of recommended courses in New Zealand. 'This true links,' the writer, Nigel Wall, enthused, 'although tatty and struggling for funds, is a remarkable example of how great land will always deliver great golf (and for just ten bucks).'

info

The 11th
Par 4
353 metres

Southland Golf Club
Links Road
Invercargill
Tel (03) 213 0208
www.nzgolfcourses.co.nz/users/web22_southland

Photography Credits

Photographs supplied courtesy of: p.13 Destination Northland; p.15 spin360.co.nz; p.16 Carrington Resort; p.17 Carrington Resort; p.19 Kauri Cliffs; p.21 Kauri Cliffs; p.23 Kauri Cliffs; pp.24–25 Niels Schipper; p.26 Destination Northland; p.27 Graeme Matthews; p.29 (top) Waitangi Golf Club; p.29 (bottom) Destination Northland; p.31 Graeme Matthews; p.33 Graeme Matthews; p.35 Niels Schipper; pp.36–37 Niels Schipper; p.39 South Head Golf Club; p.40 Tom Hyde; p.43 Huapai Golf Club; pp.44–45 Niels Schipper; p.48 Tom Hyde; p.50 & 51 Titirangi Golf Club; p.53 Ross Bryon; p.55 Niels Schipper; p.57 Remuera Golf Club; p.59 Niels Schipper; p.60 Howick Golf Club; p.62 Formosa Golf Resort; p.65 Niels Schipper; p.68 Niels Schipper; p.71 Murray Glasgow; p.73 Waikato Times; pp.74–75 Lakes Resort; p.77 D. Veitch, Crown Copyright, Department of Conservation, 1975; p.79 Tauranga Golf Club; p.81 Graeme Matthews; p.83 Te Puke Golf Club; p.84 Kiwi360; p.86 Whakatane Golf Club; p.88 Ohope International Golf Club; p.90 Springfield Golf Club; p.91 Gould Photographics; p.93 Rotorua Golf Club; p.95 Horsham Downs Golf Club; p.96 Hamilton Golf Club; p.99 Narrows Golf Club; p.100 Narrows Golf Club; p.102 Jamie Moore, WebSpring; p.104 Niels Schipper; p.106 Gray Clapham; p.108 Maraenui Golf Club; p.110 Napier Golf Club; p.112 Cape Kidnappers; p.113 Cape Kidnappers; p.114 Cape Kidnappers; p.116 Cape Kidnappers; p.118 Hastings Golf Club; pp.120–121 Wairakei International; p.123 Wairakei International; p.124 Taupo Golf Club; p.129 APN/Sarah Ivey; p.131 Graeme Matthews; pp.132–133 Niels Schipper; p.136 Tim Hales/Photosport; p.138 South Taranaki District Council; p.140 Niels Schipper; p.141 Barry Johnston; pp.142–143

Niels Schipper; p.145 Icon SMI/Photosport; p.148 Manawatu Golf Club; p.150 Nick Cooper; pp.152 & 153 Paraparaumu Beach Golf Club; p.155 Icon SMI/Photosport; p.156 Titahi Golf Club; p.158 Aratoi: Wairarapa Museum of Art and History; p.160 Masterton Golf Club; p.162 Martinborough Golf Club; p.164 Niels Schipper; p.166 David Hamilton, www.photonz.co.nz; p.168 Hutt Golf Club; p.171 David Hamilton, www.photonz.co.nz; p.172 Graeme Wilson/Nelson Golf Club; p.173 Niels Schipper; p.175 Jim Harding/Hedgehog House; p.176 Clearwater Resort; p.178 Hannah Johnston; p.180 Windsor Golf Club; p.182 Niels Schipper; p.185 Dean MacKenzie/Russley Golf Club; p.187 Templeton Golf Club; p.189 Niels Schipper; p.191 Terrace Downs; p.193 Greymouth Golf Club; p.195 Niels Schipper; p.199 North Otago Golf Club; p.201 Niels Schipper; p.203 G.O'Brien; p.205 Jonathan Elkin; p.207 Niels Schipper; p.208 & 210 Arrowtown Golf Club; p.211 Destination Queenstown; p.213 Millbrook Resort; p.214 Destinatination Queenstown; p.215 Queenstown Golf Club; p.217 Destination Queenstown; p.218 Jack's Point; p.221 Graham Dainty, Photo Art Fiordland; pp.224–225 Andy Radka.